The Economic System

CONSULTING EDITOR | **DONALD DEWEY**
Columbia University

THE
ECONOMIC
SYSTEM
by
Roger Weiss

UNIVERSITY OF CHICAGO

RANDOM HOUSE | NEW YORK |

INTRODUCTION

The introduction to economics is usually made with a thick
textbook filled with descriptions of all the economic
institutions of our time. The needs of general education
and of courses that integrate economic thinking with
political thinking call for a short statement of principles.
Most of the available studies were developed for adult
education, and although they have the virtue of popularity,
they suffer the defect of superficiality. The model of a
short statement of economics has been F. H. Knight's *The
Economic Organization,* written more than thirty years
ago. However, this work is, in some respects, too difficult
for beginning students and is not sufficiently comprehensive
for an introduction to the whole subject of economics.
The Economic System was written with the intention of
remedying these defects while holding to the purpose and
method of its model. Acknowledgment of a heavy
debt is gratefully made.

Roger Weiss
Chicago, Illinois
October, 1968

CONTENTS

The Economic System

CHAPTER I

Social Economic Organization and Its Four Primary Functions

The affluent society has not yet eliminated economic problems from our urgent concern. Some would have us believe that we have experienced a "triple revolution" that has simultaneously ended the economic problem of scarcity and created want through automation—by eliminating the jobs of the unskilled. Thus the economic problems have been solved and the political problem of adjusting the benefits equitably among the different groups remains. There is convincing evidence that automation is not steadily eliminating jobs, just as there is convincing evidence that however affluent we are, our economic problems have not disappeared. The balance-of-payments problem, the threat of inflation caused by the conflicting demands that are made on the domestic economy for output for consumption, investment,

and the need for resources for armament, the conflict between fighting the war against poverty at home and fighting
the war abroad—"guns or butter" as the older slogan put it
—all demonstrate that the economic problem of choice between conflicting uses for scarce resources endures.

The Definition of Economics

Economics is the study of the social organization of these
scarce resources for the production of the goods and services
that make up national income. If the resources were not
scarce, there would be no problem in organization—one
way would be as good as another, for efficient organization
would be unnecessary. In a society of abundance there is
no cost for wasting resources.

Definitions of economics that distinguish this study from
the study of economizing behavior are not easy to make.
There are social aspects of work and there are economic
aspects of leisure; the coffee break and the unremunerative
occupations that people often choose are aspects of work
that are "noneconomic." The economic aspects of leisure
can be illustrated by common examples. To what extent is
social life based on equal exchanges? In other words, to
what extent must an invitation to a party be reciprocated
if an individual is to be invited again? A second example
is the implicit valuation of leisure time. From the study of
prices charged by parking lots located at various distances
from a central downtown area, we can calculate a precise
measure of the price commuters are willing to pay for each
five minutes they save by utilizing the more proximate lots.

The decline of railways in the face of air transport is another example of the degree to which people place an economic value on their leisure time.

. The border between economic and noneconomic activity is further blurred by the difficulty in making clear distinctions. When we cook our meals at home, our labor is not entered in the ordinary measures of national income. When we hire a maid to cook for us, her services are added to the national income. When we buy a piece of furniture, we are making an economic transaction in the definitions used to measure national income. When we make the furniture for ourselves, our labor is not counted. The definition of economic activity usually includes what is sold in a market. Thus the maid and the furniture are economic; cooking and making furniture for oneself are not. The distinction is not a meaningful one, however; the "real" values of the food and the furniture may be the same.

The science of economics is distinct from the concrete processes of production, distribution, and consumption in much the same way as food chemistry is distinct from cooking. A good cook may be totally ignorant of the chemical processes he is employing, just as a good food chemist may be a poor cook. An economist may not be able to manage an automobile factory, just as a good businessman may have only the most simple notions about what affects the demand for his product or for all products in the economy. Economics is usually concerned with the social processes of organization. Therefore it is more likely to study the automobile industry than the Ford Motor Company; it will be concerned more with total employment than with the number of welders.

Advantages and Disadvantages of Specialization

The need to study social organization arises in a world of specialization. If each person lived self-sufficiently on an isolated farm, economic decisions would all be made within the household. Each household would employ the engineering sciences to determine how to obtain the best yields, how to construct the best equipment, and so on. The division of labor, whereby each person specializes and depends on others for the goods he consumes, requires complex organizations for coordinating the activities of the many cooperating agents of production. The study of economics arises from the advantages of specialization; the importance of specialization was recognized in the first comprehensive modern work on economics, Adam Smith's *Wealth of Nations*, published in the year 1776.

When Thomas Paine spoke of the advantages of society, he used the example of building a house.

Four or five [men] united would be able to raise a tolerable dwelling in the midst of a wilderness, but one man might labor out the common period of life without accomplishing anything; when he had felled his timber, he would not remove, nor erect it after it was removed; hunger in the meantime would urge him from his work and every different want call him a different way.[1]

Here is a society in which men cooperate in production but do not practice division of labor. The same situation can be observed in Malayan fishing communities, where many men labor in common and divide the catch. There is division of

[1] Thomas Paine, *Common Sense* (Indianapolis, Ind.: Liberal Arts Press, 1953), p. 5.

labor between fishermen and other people, but there is little division of labor among fishermen. The need for organization arises in societies where the tasks performed by the cooperating persons are different. Thus Adam Smith's pin factory represents a higher level of specialization. Each pin maker spends his time at a different operation—one draws wire, another cuts it into lengths, another sharpens the point, another forms the blunt tips, and so on. The complexity of organizing tasks within this factory is greater than that of organizing Paine's cooperative neighbors. Paine's neighbors might be self-sufficient except in the occasional building of a house. The pin maker cannot even make a pin by himself; his task is only one of many in the pin-making process. The organization of society as a whole evinces the greatest complexity. Present-day specialization has been carried to the point where even farmers are not self-sufficient with regard to the food they eat; the Iowa farmer probably buys his milk, eggs, bread, and meat from the nearest grocery store.

When specialization is carried this far, what are the means by which a society coordinates the thousands of activities to ensure that the output of steel is adequate for the needs of pin makers and the output of pins is adequate for the needs of clothing makers? What determines how many acres of corn ought to be planted by farmers who will be selling corn to processors whose products include starch, salad oil, syrup, and animal feeds?

The gains from specialization are clear; total output rises as tasks are given to workers whose training and experience raise productivity over the productivity of unspecialized workers. But there are losses as well. The household loses its self-sufficiency; each household becomes increasingly dependent on the proper functioning of the whole productive mechanism. Dislocations, caused by war, power failures, and strikes in such key industries as petroleum, stevedoring, shipping, and transportation quickly affect a multitude of other industries and workers. Even if the smooth working of the complex system could be counted on when increasing specialization and interdependence made the problems of coordination greater, there would be certain psychological losses from specialization. Repetitive tasks performed in a large organization deprive the individual of a sense of the whole process and limit his personal contacts and responsibility not only within the organization but often in society as well. The crowding of industrial workers in the growing cities of the world recalls Jefferson's passionate warning:

Those who labor in the earth are the chosen people of God . . . whose breasts he has made his peculiar deposit for substantial and genuine virtue. . . . Corruption of morals in the mass of cultivators is a phenomenon of which no age nor nation has furnished an example. It is the mark set on those who, not looking up to heaven, to their own soil and industry, as does the husbandman, for their subsistence, depend for it on the casualties and caprice of customers. Dependence begets subservience and venality, suffocates the germ of virtue, and prepares fit tools for the designs of ambition.[2]

Adam Smith made the same point:

In the progress of the division of labour, the employment of the far greater part of those who live by labour, that is, of the great body of the people, comes to be confined to a few very simple operations, frequently to one or two. But the understandings of the greater part of men are necessarily formed by their

[2] Adrienne Koch and William Peden, eds., *The Life and Selected Writings of Thomas Jefferson* (New York: Modern Library, 1944), p. 280.

ordinary employments. The man whose whole life is spent in performing a few simple operations . . . has no occasion to exert his understanding, or to exercise his invention . . . he naturally loses, therefore, the habit of such exertion, and generally becomes as stupid and ignorant as it is possible for a human creature to become.[3]

The famous industrial engineer, Frederick W. Taylor, stated this thought in another way:

Now one of the very first requirements for a man who is fit to handle pig iron as a regular occupation is that he shall be so stupid and so phlegmatic that he more nearly resembles in his mental make-up the ox than any other type. The man who is mentally alert and intelligent is for this very reason entirely unsuited to what would, for him, be the grinding monotony of work of this character.[4]

Why then do we continue to specialize? Why does the household produce an ever smaller number of the things it consumes? The answer lies in the efficiency of division of labor. Ten pin makers subdividing the tasks can produce much more than ten times the number of pins that one pin maker can make alone and still many times more pins than someone untrained in pin making could turn out. The specialization that is present in ant and termite colonies is determined by structural differences within the species. The specialization of humans may depend on differences of talent to some extent, but to an equal extent this specialization depends on the artificial creation of social organization.

The advantages of specialization derive from several

[3] Adam Smith, *Wealth of Nations* (New York: Modern Library, 1937), p. 734.
[4] Frederick Winslow Taylor, *The Principles of Scientific Management* (New York: Norton, 1967), p. 59.

sources. Innate or acquired abilities are not uniformly distributed among people. Women seem to have greater manual dexterity in assembling parts than men; the Mohawk Indians have remarkable agility in working at heights on the construction of suspension bridges. Few of us have the capacity for theoretical physics; yet one of the greatest physicists is said to have confessed to John Maynard Keynes that he had thought of becoming an economist but gave up the idea because the subject was too difficult.[5] One of the rarest capacities is the ability to provide effective leadership, and one of the greatest advantages of division of labor is the possibility of following the direction of superior leaders.

The uneven distribution of natural resources and climate gives rise to division of labor. Fishing, coffee, tea, cotton, rubber, sugar, and mineral (e.g., tin, coal, copper, and iron) industries are found in certain places favored by nature. The exploitation of these locations calls for specialization of the labor force employed.

More interesting is the possibility of the perfection of skills through repetition and experience that division of labor makes possible. Practice makes perfect and the division of labor permits practice. Rapid reading, speed and accuracy in typing, and operating a busy telephone switchboard all require learning and the steady practice that only the specialist can bring to these tasks.

[5] An example of innate ability is reported by a proud father:

> Once we had to fit a new garboard plank to *Shrew* [the name of a sailboat] . . . it was a really tricky place, with all kinds of curve and twist and bevel—the sort of place where an average shipwright would ruin two or three planks before he got the right fit. Ted looked at it, planed the wood, looked at it again, and did some more planing. Then he put it to the hull, and it went in perfectly . . . his eye and his hands were so well connected.

The New Yorker, August 26, 1967, p. 42.

Adam Smith pointed out another gain from division of labor—it eliminates the loss of time in changing locations and tools as the worker changes tasks. The modern assembly line makes this saving possible—the worker remains in one spot and performs one task; the product moves from worker to worker as it is assembled.

Division of labor permits the development of specialized machinery and tools. With an automatic welder, Japanese shipyard workers can weld in one day what skilled men would take months to do. But to justify the investment in the welding machine, a large output of ships is required—larger than that produced by many other yards. Thus division of labor and the use of specialized machines depend on a large scale of output in one enterprise. This is the famous proposition of Adam Smith: "Division of labor is limited by the extent of the market."

We have already mentioned the personal cost of specialization. There is also a social cost of coordinating the complex organization created by specialization. John K. Galbraith has described Henry Ford assembling cars himself in his own garage. When an order came in, Ford could walk over to the Dodge brothers' garage and tell them what kind of motor to build for the car. If he began in the morning, he could complete the car by evening if the motor was finished in time. Today's car requires several weeks to schedule through the assembly lines. The procedure involves a complicated system of tickets that call for the specified colors, auxiliary equipment, and body styles, each delivered to the appropriate subassembly department where the appropriate parts take their place in the many lines that converge into the completed automobile. A mistake will lead to a pink top on a green body or some other anomaly. A missing part may shut down the entire line and idle hundreds or thousands of workers. The cost of co-ordinating the complex manufacturing enterprise is very great and probably rises much faster than other costs as the enterprise gets larger. Although Henry Ford knew what his inventory of wheels in the garage was at every moment, a huge company like Westinghouse found that several weeks were required to process an order for a small motor to be shipped from an inventory of goods in warehouses across the country. If a warehouse ran out of motors, a time-consuming search was necessary to obtain a motor from another warehouse. The development of computers has made possible a great saving in time through *centralizing* the inventory control in one location. Every order is sent to Pittsburgh, where the information store locates the motor and transmits shipping instructions to the appropriate ware-house. The massive volume of paperwork necessary to keep inventory records up to date for each of the thousands of products produced in different plants and shipped from many different locations in the country would be a large expense, whatever the method of record-keeping. However, this paperwork is necessary in order to coordinate produc-tion with demand. The use of computers to store masses of information may make possible an otherwise unmanageable scale of organization, even though the cost of these systems is very great.

Interdependence

The division of labor caused by separating the household, where output is consumed, from the productive enterprise brings people into a greater dependence on distant markets and economic decisions made at a distance from themselves. The development of synthetic rubber hurts the peasant farmer in Malaya, and a strike of workers in a carburetor factory can force a ball bearing manufacturer to shut his plant; both products are used in the manufacture of an automobile. Increasing interdependence makes smooth coordination of all the parts of the system more critical and puts more pressure on the central government to step in when anything goes wrong. No wonder that writers from Aristotle to Jefferson have praised the stability and independence of people in a society composed of small farmers. Truckers, longshoremen, railroad workers, and steel workers can idle millions of workers through strikes that last for a month or two; the failure of one electrical relay in northern New York put millions of city dwellers in darkness, crippled street traffic, elevators, factories, and telephones, silenced the television sets of several cities, and affected the birth rate.

The increased productive capacity of a society whose members specialize cannot be realized without a mechanism that coordinates the separate but interdependent activities of the various productive units. Over a hundred years ago, the French journalist Frédéric Bastiat described the complexity of the problem of coordination:

On entering Paris . . . I said to myself: There are one million human beings here who would die in a few days if provisions of all sorts did not flow toward this vast metropolis. The imagination is staggered to appreciate the immense multiplicity of objects which ought to enter tomorrow past the city gates without which its inhabitants would die in convulsions of famine, riots and pillaging. Yet all are asleep at this moment without their peaceful sleep being troubled an instant by the idea of such a frightening prospect. On the other hand, 80 provinces have worked today, without coordination or understanding to provision Paris. How each day does it come out right, neither more nor less, on this gigantic market? What is the ingenious and secret force which presides with surprising regularity over movements so complicated, each regulated by so carefree a faith on which depends life and well being? [6]

The complexity of the tasks of coordination can also be seen in the "input-output" studies of Wassily Leontieff. Eighty-two industries have been classified and the output of each industry going to each other industry has been determined (see Table 1). Thus each dollar of automobile output requires nine cents of steel to be purchased directly by the automobile industry. But the other materials going into automobiles also require inputs of steel and when these indirect requirements of steel are added to the nine cents of direct requirements, the total amount of steel that is needed to produce a dollar's worth of an automobile is twenty cents. A dollar of additional petroleum output requires an additional output of one cent's worth of chemicals to supply all the direct and indirect requirements. The iron and steel industry uses three cents of chemicals in each dollar's worth of output and the chemical industry uses three cents' worth of iron and steel (directly and indirectly) in each dollar's worth of its output. It is no wonder that an economist writes:

The institutions of private enterprise leave the main initiative in economic affairs to a number of independent corporations which have developed a motivation of their own—a pursuit of *success*

[6] Frédéric Bastiat, "Il n'y a pas de principes absolus," in *Sophismes Economiques* (Paris: Guillaumin et Cie., 1854).

Table 1
Total Requirements (Direct and Indirect) Per Dollar
of Delivery to Final Demand, 1958, Selected Industries

	OTHER AGRICUL- TURAL PRODUCTS	CRUDE PETRO- LEUM	CHEMICALS AND SELECTED CHEMICAL PRODUCTS	PRIMARY IRON AND STEEL MANUFAC- TURES	MOTOR VEHICLES
Other Agricultural Products	0.11	.006	.01	.009	.006
Crude Petroleum and Natural Gas	0.03	1.03	.05	.015	.009
Chemicals and Selected Chemical Products	0.07	0.01	1.27	.03	.02
Primary Iron and Steel Manufactures	0.005	.008	.03	1.32	.20
Motor Vehicles	0.005	.003	.004	.007	1.43

SOURCE: *Survey of Current Business*, November, 1964, pp. 26–29.

NOTE: Each industry represents the output required, directly and indirectly, from the industry named at the beginning of the row for each dollar of delivery to final demand by the industry named at the head of the column.

which includes but is not bounded by the mere pursuit of profit . . . the interplay of the policies of these independent corporations cannot be relied upon to secure . . . a consistent pattern of development . . . a national "plan" is now seen to be necessary to coordinate their activities.[7]

In other words, in an economy with eighty-two industries selling to eighty-two industries and consumers of final products, Mrs. Robinson believes private decision-making cannot

[7] Joan Robinson, "Socialist Affluence," in *Socialism, Capitalism and Economic Growth* (Cambridge, England: Cambridge University Press, 1967), p. 177.

make consistent decisions about expanding production. When the chemical industry expands, steel production will not be changed by the appropriate amount. Mrs. Robinson believes that only a central direction of all industry can avoid the mistakes of leaving decisions to be made by each of the many enterprises in each of the eighty-two broad industrial groupings.

How is output determined in our world to ensure that "each day it comes out right, neither more nor less"? What is the social mechanism for keeping the units of enterprise and consumption in continual adjustment with one another? Three types of organization are discussed below: traditional, autocratic, and exchange.

Types of Organization

1. Traditional, Status, or Caste Systems. In societies that experience little technological change, organization through assignment of functions by birth can give a rather stable order to economic activities, even though considerable division of labor obtains. At the extreme, the occupation of each person may be rigidly prescribed with the sanction of religion, and so long as the initial distribution of occupations does not violate the most elemental requirements (so that a minimum number of the people are engaged in farming, for instance), the system can function— if not efficiently, at least stably. There might be so many shoemakers that each one barely stays alive and so few lawyers that each lives in a villa with many servants. The economy might slowly change as different products change in relative scarcity through depletion of resources, soil exhaustion or erosion, changes in climate, and slow changes in available technology and capital resources. However, in such structured societies, decisions are made by the ruling tradition of what is the proper occupation for members according to the caste into which they are born. In the structured society of nineteenth-century England, the younger sons of nobility might choose the ministry, law, or the military for a career; some entered banking and perhaps certain other "respectable" businesses, but they avoided musical performance, painting, and many lucrative occupations. Even the freest society has certain cultural sanctions on the choice of occupations.

2. The Autocratic or Militaristic System. Instead of decisions about occupation and division of labor being made "by tradition," suppose they were made through a centralized dictatorship that was in control of the entire productive system through ownership of the means of production and that utilized (as in some ancient societies) the laboring population as slaves. A picture of such a social order may be found in the story of Joseph in Egypt after the chattels of the people were turned over to Pharaoh in exchange for the grain stored up by Joseph against the lean years.

In our time the socialist economies of the U.S.S.R. and its satellites have created a planning and decision authority responsible for prescribing the amounts of goods of all kinds to be produced in the state-owned units of production. A target is fixed for each enterprise, indicating not only the expected output but also the labor, machinery, and materials that should be allocated to the enterprise for use in production. The sum of all such planned outputs is then the total output and the total resources required for the economy. Fixing targets and allocating productive resources require extremely detailed information; central direction of a complex and changing economy therefore requires an efficient flow of information to and from the center and a method of rewards and penalties for enforcing orders issued from the center. The problems confronting the central authority are not difficult to anticipate. The single plan, so difficult to construct (depending as it does on the fine adjustment of all the component pieces in the economy), is very difficult to alter; any one change requires hundreds of others. Even where the need is obvious, the plan will resist alterations. Production targets must be carefully negotiated. The central authority will want them set high so as to maximize output from the available resources but not so high that underfulfillment will result in shortages and production breakdowns in other areas. The producing unit will want them set low so that the rewards for fulfillment will be attainable. In addition there are problems of determining which outputs are most highly valued by consumers, although in practice the problems are avoided largely by ignoring consumer preferences.[8]

3. *The Exchange System.* During the rapid development of the eighteenth and nineteenth centuries, the economies of Western countries were not organized by any conscious authority of the state or any private group. There was a "free-enterprise system," or what is also called the free-price system, regulated by what Adam Smith brilliantly

---

[8] Writing seventy-five years before the Russian experiment in central planning, J. S. Mill could not conceive of "one or a few human beings, howsoever selected . . . [being] qualified to adapt each person's work to his capacity, and proportion each person's remuneration to his merits." From *Principles of Political Economy* (London: Longmans, 1909), Book II, Chapter 1, p. 213.

described as "the invisible hand." [9] It was a system that was never formally instituted but that operated for centuries without anyone being aware of it. Producers and consumers made their own decisions, guided by the prices prevailing in the thousands of product and resource markets. The economic system of eighteenth- and nineteenth-century capitalism, described by Adam Smith and Karl Marx, was one of private ownership of productive resources and private use of these resources for selling goods and services.[10]

This discussion of the workings of a decentralized, competitive free-price system does not imply that our economy, or any other that has existed in history, is without problems

[9] See Adam Smith, *Wealth of Nations* (New York: Modern Library, 1937), p. 423:

> As every individual, therefore, endeavors as much as he can both to employ his capital in the support of industry, and so to direct that industry that its produce may be of the greatest value; every individual necessarily labours to render the annual revenue of the society as great as he can. He generally, indeed, neither intends to promote the public interest, nor knows how much he is promoting it. . . . By directing . . . industry in such a manner as its produce may be of the greatest value, he intends only his own gain, and he is in this, as in many other cases, led by an invisible hand to promote an end which was no part of his intention. Nor is it always the worse for the society that it was no part of it. By pursuing his own interest he frequently promotes that of the society more effectually than when he really intends to promote it. I have never known much good done by those who affected to trade for the public good. It is an affectation, indeed, not very common among merchants, and very few words need be employed in dissuading them from it.

[10] Another type of social organization can be conceived that is neither traditional, autocratic, nor decentralized with free exchange. Various applications of communal, cooperative, syndicalist, or kibbutz organization have been advocated and have been attempted with varying degrees of success. In this general form, individuals associate themselves voluntarily in small units whose direction is democratic. Coordinating the individual units requires higher bodies like representative or confederated congresses, perhaps with subordinate agencies to draft plans and administer the coordination.

—problems that are often serious. The problems of monopoly, population growth, unemployment, and poverty provoked the thinking that led to the development of modern economic theory in the late eighteenth century and the first half of the nineteenth century. The strongest defenders of laissez-faire[11] governmental policies wrote with full awareness of inequality, poverty, and the population problem. There are eminent economists who call themselves socialists, from John Stuart Mill to Joan Robinson; others who support sweeping measures of governmental intervention, from John Maynard Keynes to Paul Samuelson; as well as those who favor minimal (but still considerable) intervention by government, from Adam Smith to Milton Friedman.

When comparing actual economies, we have no trouble identifying the wastes and inefficiencies of centrally planned and free-market economies. It is a mistake, however, to regard the study of economics as concerning only the choice between capitalism and socialism. Decentralization of the decision-making process has many features that, with ingenuity, might be adopted by socialist planners. Indeed, Russian economists proposed such a reform in August 1964, and earlier, various economists in satellite countries elaborated ambitious decentralization schemes.[12] At the same

[11] "Laissez faire" is the term used to indicate a governmental policy of "let alone," or noninterference in the private-enterprise system.
[12] See *The New York Times*, August 18, 1964:

Academician Trapeznikov advocated a system of bonuses, taxes, fines and flexible prices and greater leeway for decision making by plant managers instead of detailed planning supervision by central planning authorities.

Mr. Trapeznikov made no secret of the fact that many elements were borrowed from the West. As practices worth emulating he mentioned tax exemptions on the share of a corporation's income reinvested into research and development as a device for stimulating technical progress and the system of high fines paid by suppliers

time, the growing government sector of Western economies has brought greater importance to centralized decision-making. This is not to say that Russia and the West will join one another in a happy economic compromise some day but that the forms of market organization can be studied independently of the ownership of resources.

The Four Main Functions of an Economic System

The general task of organizing the economic activity of a society may be divided into a number of basic functions. These are in fact very much interconnected and overlapping, but the distinction is useful as an aid to discussing the structure and workings of the existing economic order, both descriptively and critically. The first function is to decide what goods and services are to be produced and in what amounts. The society must have a way of setting standards or priorities—a scale of values in choosing the products or services that it is to engage in making. The second function is that of organizing the production of the various goods and services, of choosing the combination of resources that will be used to make each one. The third function is to distribute or divide the goods produced among the members of the society. The fourth is providing for the increase of output in the future.

1. The Function of Fixing Standards. If men were self-sufficient, production decisions would be made by each man

---

for delays in delivery of goods. Such delays have been a perennial problem in the Soviet economy.

. . . a rate of interest on capital should be introduced into the Soviet economy. Such a charge would be designed to speed the turnover of operating capital which is now frozen in excess supply stocks and to encourage factory managers to make more efficient use of their plant and equipment.

for himself. Where production is a social process, a mechanism for expressing the relative priorities of the importance of different sorts of goods must be employed to guide in the allocation of productive resources. Individual wants must be ranked so that consumers can choose among different products available. At the same time, these individual preferences must be combined in a way that indicates, for the whole society, the best relative proportions of goods and services in the total output. This function calls for a massive market research or public opinion survey organization.

2. *The Function of Organizing Production.* Suppose one knew what products were desired and in what proportions. Decisions would still have to be made concerning the best manner of combining resources for the different outputs. Should dresses be made in factories or in the small household workshop? How large should each unit of production be? Should grapes be picked by hand or by machine? Should the farm enterprise be coordinated under the same management as the retail enterprise or should it merely be linked with the factories processing farm products? A society must have a means of answering these questions that affect the organization and scale of enterprises; it must determine as well the proper combination of resources to be employed in each activity and the choice among the various technologies to be employed in producing each product.

3. *The Function of Distribution.* If we knew what to produce and how to produce, we would still have to determine how to distribute the products among the cooperating agents of production. The term "distribution" in ordinary press usage usually means the system by which goods are moved from factories to consumers, through a network of jobbers, wholesalers, and retailers. However, following the

older usage, we speak of distribution as the process by which society decides what portion of the total output should go to each productive agent—different types of labor, management, landowners, and lenders of capital. If each man worked entirely independently, the share of society's income that he would be given would be determined by how much he produced. Distribution would be determined by the first two functions. Where production is in the form of an assembly line, how much of the product is made by the person who installs the tires, how much by the person who installs the brakes, and how much by the foreman, the president of the company, and the salesman is not obvious. Still another question is how much of the product *should* go to each person.

4. Economic Progress. By using a portion of current output for the production of capital goods (that is, machinery and buildings), we add to the productive capacity of the economy and thereby increase future output of goods and services. The act of reducing present consumption to release productive resources is called saving; the act of employing the saved resources in building the plant and equipment is called investment. Sometimes these two facets of economic growth are determined by the same person—for example, when a farmer plows under a crop to increase the fertility of the soil. But sometimes saving and investment are performed by different individuals—for example, when an individual saves in order to buy a bond issued by a city to erect a new school building. Investment adds to the stock of capital, either by adding to the supply of machines and buildings of the kind we already have or by adding to and improving productive capacity for the production of new products through the utilization of new technologies.

A decision to save is a choice between present and future consumption; the higher future income that is made possible by adding to the stock of capital requires sacrifice of present consumption.

The first three functions relate to what is called stationary economics, or statics, referring to an economy whose underlying conditions—population, technology, and capital stock—remain stable. An increase in the preference for one product implies a decrease in the preference for some other. The problems studied under these assumptions isolate the operation of the economy in allocating and distributing incomes and in organizing production. These functions operate in a world of changing resources, wealth, and technology. The problems introduced by the conditions of capital accumulation, population growth, saving, and technological change are "dynamic" problems. Analysis of problems under assumptions of static conditions is often convenient in order to isolate just those influences with which we are most concerned. Thus the economics of stationary conditions is useful even in a world of steady change, much as the physics of falling bodies, whose laws are valid only in a vacuum, gives predictions that are useful in the real world of atmospheric pressure.

Economic theory, like any theory, is "a method rather than a doctrine, an apparatus of the mind, a technique of thinking, which helps its possessor to draw correct conclusions" about the cause-and-effect relations of events in the real world. Why, then, will two competent economists disagree in recommending a course of action to solve a problem? Sometimes the reason is that they place different values on the intended or unintended by-products of the action. Thus although they may agree that the elimination of government rent controls will permit rents to rise and that the available supply of housing will be better allocated and better maintained thereby, they may disagree on other effects: landlords will have larger incomes and tenants will spend more on rent. In other cases, freedom, higher output, and efficiency may be the alternatives to equality. The choice between these alternatives requires criteria other than output or efficiency.

At other times disagreement may rest on, as Mill said, a comparison of what exists and has manifest flaws with an alternative, which, untried, exists in the ideal and has its flaws concealed. We must compare commensurable items— not the ideal of one with the actual of another. Finally, disagreement may be caused by differences over facts. For example, in discussing unemployment we may need to know whether the unemployed are displaced, immobile victims of automation, whether they are shifting jobs and desire an intervening period in which to move, whether they are unskilled workers migrating from backward, sharecropping farms to industrial cities of the North, or whether they are victims of racial prejudice searching for jobs for which their skills qualify them.

CHAPTER II

The Price System
and the
Economic Process

In this chapter the price system is examined as a means of organizing the complex economic decisions of society and of coordinating the responses to these decisions.

Modern Economic Organization, an "Automatic" System

The exchange or free-enterprise system permits a highly sensitive coordination to take place without conscious design or control, employing the invisible hand of private motivation and activity. Although lacking a plan from above, the system operates with remarkable speed. Innumerable conflicts of private interest are constantly resolved without strikes or government intervention, and the bulk of the working population is kept generally occupied, each person ministering to the wants of an unknown multitude and having his own wants satisfied by another multitude equally vast and unknown.

Price, the Guide and Regulator: The Price System

Prices are determined by the interplay of supply and demand in each market and serve two functions. They are information signals that indicate the relative value of each object passing through the market—raw materials and labor services, as well as intermediate and finished products. They also provide rewards for employing resources to the best advantage. Resource owners endeavor to find employment where rewards are the highest, and entrepreneurs attempt to employ resources in the production of items whose value gives them the maximum return over the value of the productive resources they must employ. Consumers at one end of the production cycle spend their money incomes on the goods for which they have preference at the values for which the various goods are offered. Where consumer preferences rise, demand will exceed production. Sellers will react by raising prices. The higher prices will restrain consumers somewhat by prompting them to favor products whose prices have not risen. But the profit afforded by selling the product with the higher price will attract producers to shift resources to the production of this product. Thus the preferences of consumers will pull (reward) resources to the uses of highest value, indicated by the higher prices (as signals) in the favored markets. At the other end of the production cycle, the resource owner who receives payments for his services enters the market for finished products as a consumer, completing the cycle of the circular flow of income.

The price system is thus a method of expressing preferences—of choosing. Consumers with money incomes have powers of choosing in proportion to the size of their incomes. But to express preferences is not enough; the economy must be organized to respond to the preferences. Organization takes place in the price system when resources respond to the profit motive and move to activities where profits are greatest—that is, where consumers have expressed preferences for certain goods, indicated by the higher prices of these goods. Without the response of buyers and sellers to price, the price system would be no more than an ingenious voting device, and in Soviet planned economies, the price system often is just that. The planning agency, having determined the output for a certain product, adjusts the price of that product to the level at which demand will create no shortages. In order for consumer preferences to guide the use of resources in a socialist economy, the planning board must move resources *as if it were* motivated by profits.

As a democratic mechanism for expressing preferences, the price system has many advantages over the political balloting system. For one thing, many different types of preferences can be accommodated simultaneously (for Rolls Royces and Volkswagens). For another, the economic "balloting" is so decentralized that voters (except where there is monopoly or powerful organization) feel that the choice is automatic. The conflicts that arise in elections for political office, conducted according to majority rule, do not appear in the competitive market.

In such a brief sketch, the price system (or enterprise or

free-enterprise system) seems quite simple, and its operation appears to be altogether beneficent. Its smooth operation, in keeping the allocation of resources in line with consumer preferences, would seem to be clearly implied from the brief description of the economic voting mechanism that resolves disputes "automatically." If this were true there would be little need for the 14,000 economists who belong to the American Economic Association, much less the millions of amateur economists who make economic decisions at each national and local election. Before we can understand the problems of a particular form of organization, we must view its operation abstractly to see what its ideal operation would be like; only later can we deal with the details of its problems (recessions, inflation, unemployment, monopoly, low income accruing to certain groups, and so on). Although the mere willingness to discuss the price system in its ideal may well indicate a certain bias in favor of this system (at least to the degree of saying that discussion of its operation is conceivable), economic analysis can proceed in describing and analyzing without presuming to justify. Discourse between a socialist and "free-enterprise" economist is possible within the framework of this analysis and is in fact increasingly taking place as the Soviet economies are liberalizing their mode of organization. Explaining is not the same thing as justifying, in any case.

Consumption

Economics is not independent of many circumstances that are determined largely outside the economic framework. Economists take the wants or values of persons in the society as given conditions under the assumption that the ends of economic activity should be determined by the participants in the process—in any case not by economists. In a non-democratic state this need not be true; the dictator of the proletariat may very well decide what people shall have. But even if we describe "democratic" societies and assume that the ends of production should be democratically determined, we cannot ignore the extent to which people's wants are influenced by "keeping up with the Joneses" or by the hidden persuaders of advertising. At this stage we shall ignore these qualifications and describe the operation of the price system, accepting wants as consumers may express them in the market.

We must also begin by taking as given (determined outside the system) the amount of resources (natural, human, and produced) available for productive activity and the techniques that are available for putting them to work. This is not to say that the stock of resources remains constant or that a portion of current output is not invested to improve technology. All of these, resources, technology, and investment (along with wants) are influenced by our economic activities.

We agree with Adam Smith that "Consumption is the sole end and purpose of all production; and the interest of the producer ought to be attended to, only so far as it may be necessary for promoting that of the consumer." [1] Consumption must, however, be interpreted broadly. We do, in fact, choose lower incomes in order to have more leisure (some of which we need in order to be able to consume). We also

[1] Adam Smith, *Wealth of Nations* (New York: Modern Library, 1937), p. 625.

choose to reduce consumption in order to save and increase the future incomes not only of ourselves but of our children. We may build pyramids and churches, drink and dissipate our incomes, or collect old books and glass telegraph insulators. But our criteria of efficiency assume that we seek to maximize the value of consumable output with our given resources and technology. And because economists surrender their right to impose their criteria, they accept (often reluctantly) consumer valuations of comic books and popular music, although privately they may contribute to pay the deficit of the university or the symphony, which are unable to meet their expenses by selling services in the market. For some purposes distinctions are made between luxuries and necessities, but in practice today's luxuries for the rich are tomorrow's necessities for the masses; economists are just as distrustful of the distinction between luxuries and necessities as they are of the old-fashioned distinction between productive and unproductive labor. In general we must say that the productivity of a resource or the utility of a service or product can only be measured by what price the resource brings in a competitive market.

Income

We have used the word "income" without defining it. Income is the portion of current output that can be consumed without thereby incurring a reduction of future income. A portion of output must be used to replace machines and buildings that wear out; from total output this allowance for depreciation is deducted to reach net (social and personal) income. Adam Smith might better have phrased his statement: Income is the sole end and purpose of all production.

The definition of income for society can be understood by the example of defining the income of the farmer, who formerly had to set aside a portion of his harvest to store as seed for planting the next crop. If he treated his entire harvest as income, he would destroy his future income; he would "live on his capital."

There are many problems related to the measurement of income. If we look at beautiful trees in our own back yard we are not, perhaps, consuming a service. But if we go to a private park and pay admission to see beautiful trees, we are buying a service that will be income as defined by governmental statistical reports. If we eat in a restaurant, our purchase of a meal will add to income as defined by payments made in commercial establishments. But do we not enjoy some (if not more) utility from having the same meal at home? If so, a proper definition of income would have to include the value of cooking and serving a meal. Similar problems of handling services that do not pass through a market, such as home carpentry and the rental value of owner-occupied housing, face anyone who tries to define income in such a way as to be able to measure it.

The Factors of Production: Land, Labor, and Capital

What, then, is *capital?* In economics, capital is considered to be reproducible productive resources, in order to distinguish this factor from land and labor. By investing resources in education we can increase human productivity; by draining, fertilizing, and irrigating we can increase the productivity of the land. Thus human beings as well as land are capital; the productive potential of both can be increased.[2] Capital is the result of investment. From the point of view of the individual saver, capital is any instrument of debt that he might hold; some of these are in the form of an I.O.U., a mortgage, a savings or deposit account in a bank, or stocks and bonds. From a social point of view, these are *instruments* of capital and should not be counted as the tangible capital that they perhaps represent.

The measurement of capital is conceptually very difficult. Although we can easily determine the value of an apartment building when it is built in terms of the cost of the land, materials, and labor with which it was built, at a later date the value of the building will be determined by its projected future earning capacity. Because of new construction or changed demand for apartments, the projected future income may be quite different from that projected before the building was built. The value of the building at the later date may therefore be either higher or lower than the cost of the building; the value of a particular capital object is thus its "discounted expected earnings." The changing values of common stocks can be understood if they are explained as the outcome of a continual discounting of the uncertain future.

Land and the other natural resources were formerly distinguished from capital and labor in that they were viewed as "original and nonreplaceable" factors of production. A clear distinction cannot be made, however (as pointed out

---

[2] John Locke clearly had this idea in mind when, in the *Second Treatise of Government*, he distinguished between land in a state of nature and land when privately owned (sections 37, 40): the latter has been improved by the addition of labor (investment) to raise its productivity above the productivity of land in the state of nature.

above), because to a large extent, land is "created" by investment and can be destroyed in the production process if it is not carefully maintained.

The third productive factor traditionally listed is *labor.* If all labor were performed by slaves, there would be no need for discussing labor as a separate category; labor would be another form of capital. In a free market the wage of labor is set by the forces of supply and demand, as described below. Through unions, labor attempts to regulate wages by controlling its supply to an industry.

The Role of the Entrepreneur

Coordination of the factors of production within a single enterprise is performed by the entrepreneur, who hires labor, borrows capital and rents land, and makes the decisions about production. Whereas labor is paid wages, capital, interest, and land, rent, the entrepreneur receives only the residual (profit) when there is any. In modern times the entrepreneur is usually not a single person, as was most common earlier when such captains of industry as John D. Rockefeller, Henry Ford, and Andrew Carnegie built up and owned huge enterprises. To locate the entrepreneur in a giant corporate enterprise of today one must look to the shareholders of the corporation, whose reward is the residual after payment to the hired resources, labor, land, and borrowed capital. Of course the shareholder (as well as the earlier individual entrepreneur) supplies considerable amounts of capital. To this extent, what is reported as the profit of the corporation includes interest on the capital employed. However, there is no fixed guarantee that shareholders will earn a return on their investment; they there-

fore bear the ultimate uncertainty of the enterprise and per-
form the function of the entrepreneur,[3] at least as long as
the enterprise remains solvent. Under perfect competition,
the entry of new firms and the consequent increase of output will, in the long run, eliminate profit (greater than normal returns to capital) and make the special function of
entrepreneurship unnecessary—in an unchanging world.
But in the rapidly changing real world there are, at any
moment, new industries whose products are in heavy demand; here entrepreneurship organizes expansion. Older
(so-called mature) industries, if not declining, have more
stable demand and settled methods of production. In these
industries, not only are profits lower than in rapidly growing
"new" industries, but the character of management can be
said to be more administrative than entrepreneurial.

The theoretical enterprise or firm, which we shall describe
in more detail later, thus has a management appointed by
the shareholders, who act through an elected board of
directors in whom the entrepreneurial function is concentrated. The management executes and often initiates the
policies of the directors in deciding what to produce, how
to produce it, and how to combine the employed resources
of land, labor, and borrowed capital.

When Adam Smith wrote, the typical entrepreneur was
the small merchant or farmer, operating an enterprise con-
sisting of no more than ten employees. The corporation
existed only for operations whose scale was too large to
permit a small number of partners, relying on their own

[3] Joseph Schumpeter describes the function of entrepreneurship at
length in his *Theory of Economic Development* (New York: Galaxy
Books, 1961), giving credit to the captain of industry for the innovations that have revolutionized technology and organization in our
economy.

capital and their limited powers of borrowing, to amass the resources for such undertakings as building canals and roads or to engage in trade on the scale of that carried on by the British East India Company. Among the many small traders there was competition. With the scale of the "typical" enterprise greatly enlarged today, the argument is sometimes advanced that the conditions of competition have been abandoned and that the new organization of business activity is free from control by its owners, by its customers, and by its competitors—it is a self-perpetuating bureaucracy, public in character, seeking the security of its managers.[4] In a world of perfect *competition*, the profit of the enterprise tends to disappear in the process of adjusting the number of firms in each industry to the demand for their output; the character of management becomes more and more routine as the industry matures. In the world described by Professor Galbraith, the monopolistic enterprises perpetuate their profits and the management function remains highly important within the enterprise.

The Enterprise, the Price System, and the Circular Flow of Income

The individual or household enters economic activity as a supplier of resources (labor, land, or capital) and as a consumer of goods and services. Because economic activity is organized in enterprises to which individuals sell their labor and from which they buy the goods and services they consume (except in cases where we might find a subsistence farmer, wholly isolated from the rest of the economy that

[4] John K. Galbraith, *The New Industrial State* (Boston: Houghton Mifflin, 1967).

employs specialization), the household is more and more a unit of consumption and the productive enterprise is less and less a household. The family farm and the domestic workshop, where the craftsman and his family worked at a loom, are no longer typical organizations and will be ignored in this analysis, along with the government, universities, and other nonprofit employers from which many households draw income, either as employees or as beneficiaries of such transfer payments as social security. The private sector of the economy is organized through the flows of money to and from the enterprises producing goods that are sold in markets and that eventually pass into the households of those who sell services to productive enterprises. Through this two-way flow of money and incomes, total output is directed into the hands of consumers, just as the total supply of resources is directed to the enterprises that employ them in production. In Figure 1, representing the circular flow of income, the flow of money from households to retailers for goods consumed is indicated by a solid line. The retailers, in turn, pay for the goods produced by factories and farms, who, in turn, hire labor and other resources from households and pay money to them. The money flowing to households as income is spent once again for goods and services.

We can trace the flow of goods and services in these markets by the dotted circle. Households supply labor and other resources to firms (the flow from d to c); firms supply products and services to households (the flow from b to a). The individual who works for an enterprise is unlikely to buy anything that enterprise produces; typically, he spends his income for products of other industries or, at most, spends only a small part of his income on his own products.

The actual money flow diagram in an economy such as ours would have to show the flow of funds into and out of government accounts, the investment and saving expenditures of firms and households, and the many transactions among firms supplying "intermediate" or "producers'" goods —the semifinished goods that are worked on in their vari-

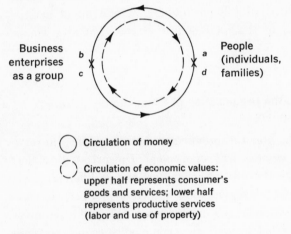

Business enterprises as a group   b   c

a   d   **People (individuals, families)**

○ Circulation of money

◌ Circulation of economic values: upper half represents consumer's goods and services; lower half represents productive services (labor and use of property)

Figure 1
The Circular Flow of Income

ous stages by different enterprises and the finished goods that are used up entirely by firms in the process of producing other goods. A more sophisticated circular flow of income diagram is included in Chapter V (Figure 5), showing not only the influence of government and saving but the manner in which the definitions of national income and gross national product relate to the less specific term "income" used here. The aggregate income shown in Figure 1 for the entire economy is the sum of the net incomes of households (d); this equals the aggregate income of firms

(b) as well as the aggregate expenditures of households for goods and services (a) and investment.

The study of how the price system organizes the flows among these households and firms focuses on two sets of prices and how they are determined: the prices of consumption goods and the prices of productive services. Together these prices influence the allocation of resources to firms, the proportions of different products in total output, and the distribution of the total output (income) among households.

Prices and the Organization of Production and Distribution

How do the prices of products and resources help in regulating the circular flow of income? The prices consumers pay indicate the relative valuations of the different goods to consumers, taken as a group, and guide producers in making decisions about what to produce. When the resources that are needed to produce a commodity cannot be hired below the price the good can be sold for, firms will reduce output or cease production. The price of a good thus tells the consumer how expensive the commodity is to produce and guides the consumer in making choices among different goods. The price also tells a producer how much the consumer is willing to pay and thus guides the producer in making decisions about which products to make.

Resource prices give the producer in a competitive industry a means of choosing among different combinations of resources in production. They thus help the producer in choosing the least costly method of using resources, the most efficient scale of output in any one plant, the location of the plant in relation to the market, and the least costly method of transporting the finished goods to the markets. There is an interaction or mutuality of determination between the prices of the finished products and the prices of the resources used in their production. If one resource becomes more valuable (if its price should rise), the cost of producing the products it is used for will rise. Eventually the price of the finished product will rise and consumers will have incentives to substitute other products. If this substitution occurs, the demand for the product, and consequently the output of the product, will fall. The employment of the resource whose price rose will fall back, and, depending on the amount of the resource that is available and the reason for its initial price rise, its price will be adjusted to the lower demand. By giving signals and incentives to those who use resources in production and to those who consume products, the price system provides a method of coordinating the demands of consumers with the availability of resources.

The prices of finished products determine the demand for resources in different industries. The demand for resources determines the incomes of the various resources. The incomes of the resources determine demands for finished products as well as the amount of savings set aside from the community's income. Interest rates are prices that guide the amount of savings and the uses to which savings are put. The price that borrowers have to pay in order to secure the use of savings determines which, among the many alternative uses, the savings will be put to; projects that cannot earn enough to pay the market rate of interest will have to be put aside. Thus the interest rate helps to organize the use of savings. The interest rate also helps to determine the amount of savings; at higher interest rates many persons will save more.

CHAPTER III

Demand,
Supply, and Price

In this chapter we will examine the relationships of demand and supply more closely, to see how prices can organize economic decisions and resource allocation.

The Market

For some products, buyers and sellers or their agents come together and actively trade in a single location. The New York Stock Exchange (where industrial common stock shares are traded), the Board of Trade, and the Mercantile Exchange (where such commodities as wheat and soybeans are bought and sold) are examples of this sort of market. In addition many products are sold in markets where sellers are located close to one another—Smithfield Market in London and Les Halles in Paris house many food wholesalers under a single roof. Frequently sellers of one product, although not under a single roof, will locate in close proximity —the many automobile rows in our country and the medieval town craftsmen who were often located on one street are examples. Finally, a market can exist with buyers and sellers scattered over several continents, connected to one another by telephones through a specialist who "makes a market" by matching telephoned orders to buy and sell. Such a market has developed for trading U.S. government bonds. In economics a market is said to exist whenever prices of a commodity are uniform and when one trade affects the prices of all.

In such a market of many buyers and sellers, price is determined by the interaction of supply and demand; price will rise or fall until the quantity supplied balances the quantity demanded at that price. At a price that is higher than equilibrium, the quantity supplied will exceed that demanded; with some product left unsold, sellers will lower prices. In a "perfect" market the same commodity will sell at the same price to all buyers; otherwise buyers will pass up the high-priced item and buy the cheaper one. Unsold products will thus drive the price down to a level at which the quantity demanded is sufficient to clear the market. This is the so-called law of supply and demand.

The analysis of supply and demand explains how prices and the allocation of resources are determined by looking at the two sides of a transaction—the buyer and the seller, whose responses are those of demand and supply. For the economy as a whole, those who consume the products are the same people as those who produce them. But with specialization, people supply labor and other services to a firm whose output is almost certainly not consumed by its own workers. Those who work to supply any one product, therefore, are not the people who demand that product. The forces that influence demand are distinct from the forces that influence supply. Let us begin by looking at demand.

DEMAND

The household, spending out of the incomes of its members, saves a portion and allocates the remainder among the different goods and services, under the constraint that it cannot (for long periods) spend more than it earns and that if it spends more on one item, it will have less to spend on others. How do prices influence the household's decisions about how much to buy of any one item? For most items, the lower the price, the more of the item that will be consumed. This is explained in two ways. At lower prices, we can afford more of the item—that is, we can consume more without giving up any other item. But also, at lower prices, we have an incentive to substitute more of the cheaper item for similar items that are now relatively more expensive. The quantity of an item that we consume is therefore a variable that is influenced by the price we pay. The relation between the quantity demanded and the price we pay is an inverse one and is pictured in Figure 2. The curve (drawn here as a straight line) that connects the amounts we would demand at different prices is called the demand curve or schedule. When we speak of the demand for a good, we usually refer to the schedule of demand—the relationship between price and the amounts demanded—keeping in the background the other forces that affect de-

mand (income, prices of related goods, and our schedule
of preferences) so that the effects of price on our demand
are isolated from the effects of the other variables. At another time we may be interested in the effects of income on
demand, and another sort of analysis will be called for.

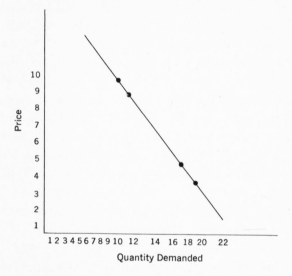

Figure 2
Hypothetical Demand for Commodity X

The *law of demand* states that the demand curve is down-
ward sloping—that the relationship between price and
quantity is inverse. The logic of this statement is plausible
and has been confirmed in the many empirical studies that
have been undertaken. In dealing with economic problems,
it is important to know not only that there is an inverse
relation but the strength of this relationship. If we lower
price 10 percent will the quantity demanded rise by 5 per-

cent or by 15 percent? The responsiveness of demand to changes in price is called *elasticity;* when the percentage change in quantity is less than the percentage change in price, demand is said to be inelastic. Demand for matches or salt is, in the range of prices normally charged, quite inelastic. If prices changed 10 or 15 percent, the quantity that consumers would seek to purchase would not change by very much. But the consumption of pie cherries might fall much more than 10 percent if the price of pie cherries rose by 10 percent when apple prices did not change. Demand for matches is inelastic; demand for pie cherries in this case is elastic. The response of consumers to price changes tells us that matches are relatively indispensable and that pie cherries have ready substitutes. The different responses to price changes show one aspect of how prices organize production—prices provide a means of indicating the strength of consumer preferences for products and a means of indicating to consumers what choices to make— for example, when to make apple pie instead of cherry pie.

SUPPLY

We assumed that prices rose 10 percent in the examples above. To know what might have caused this rise we must continue with an examination of supply. The man in the street would say that the obvious relationship between quantity supplied and price is inverse; he would tell us that a supply curve looks like the demand curve drawn above. Usually the (incorrect) explanation is that mass production always permits increased output at lower unit costs; therefore if the firm can sell more, it can afford to charge less. If this were true, we would expect prices always to be falling until only one firm was producing all the output in each industry. Common sense tells us that this cannot be (and is not) true.

If a firm found that it could sell its products for a higher price, in the very short run (what we might call immediate run) the firm would not be able to change its output at all. Production schedules are set, raw materials are ordered, and so on, and in a period that will differ for each industry, output cannot be changed, regardless of price. The correct supply curve under these conditions would be a vertical line. Suppose that we allow a period long enough for the firm to adjust its working schedules, order sufficient raw materials, and train additional workers if necessary. Most likely, the supply curve will be upward sloping in this *short-run* period. The firm is able to expand output but only by increasing cost per unit. This situation is explained by the need to raise output when some of the productive resources cannot be augmented. In a very short period the firm's plant and machinery cannot be changed, and any additions to output must be made with increased use of resources (overtime, in the case of labor). The added congestion of the plant will raise costs per unit of output, and thus the firm will be willing to increase output in the short run only if higher prices are received for its goods (see Figures 3 and 4).

If the period of adjustment is long enough, the firm can raise output by adding to plant and machinery. If this addition is possible, there is no reason why production costs need rise as output is increased. To produce twice as much, we can build a second plant with the same costs whose production costs will be the same as in the first plant. The

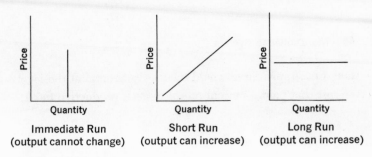

Figure 3
Supply Relationships Over Time

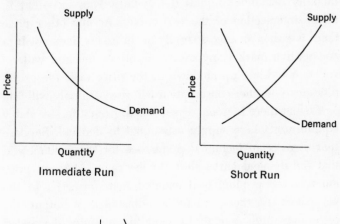

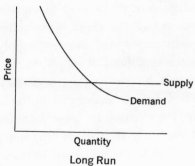

Figure 4
Demand and Supply Relationships Over Time

Demand, Supply, and Price

long-run supply curve would then be horizontal at the level of cost that paid a normal return to each productive factor.

THE EQUILIBRIUM OF DEMAND AND SUPPLY

At this point we can put together the demand and supply curves. Price in any market will come to rest where the quantity demanded equals the quantity supplied—that is, at the intersection of the two curves. At any other price there is either an excess supply or an excess demand. In a competitive market any excess supply or demand will result in a bidding up or down of the price until the excess disappears—either consumption will rise or supply will fall.

Now let there be some displacement from a former stable equilibrium where supply was equal to demand. Suppose that there is an increased preference for the product and that the demand curve shifts to the right. At every price more of the product is demanded than formerly. In the very short run there can be no adjustment of output; the price rises high enough to keep the quantity demanded where it was before the curve shifted. But as firms are able to expand output, the industry supply will shift to the right as the conditions of supply, in the short run, are met. Prices will be still higher than they were before demand shifted but not as high as in the immediate run. As sufficient time passes for new factories to be built, supply will gradually shift to its long-run position; price then will fall back to the initial equilibrium. In the adjustment described here, the industry has reacted to a change in demand by expanding output. A similar sequence of adjustments could be set out for the opposite case of demand falling and the industry shrinking in the long run.

The adjustments assume that there is "perfect" competition in the industry—that each firm is so small in relation to the whole industry that it cannot influence the industry's price by its own decisions about production. The firm takes the prevailing market price as given and makes its own decisions about output, making as much profit as it can. Another assumption is that resources are available to make the adjustments in output we have described. This assumption is not unreasonable as long as the industry and its adjustments form a small part of the whole economy. To expand output in this industry, resources are drawn from many other industries, demand for whose products might be declining slightly as preferences shift toward the products of the industry we are discussing. When we attempt to speak of the *aggregate* demand for all output, this analysis will not be valid; in a fully employed economy output either cannot increase in the short run, or it can increase only as much as new investment permits. Thus we can speak of the adjustment of output and an upward-sloping supply curve only when we speak of a relatively small sector of the economy. What is true for the part is not true for the whole.

How does this very abstract picture help us to understand the world of reality? It helps explain why, for centuries, governments have drawn their taxes from certain commodities, of which salt, matches, alcoholic beverages, tobacco, and, more recently, telephone calls and gasoline are the most important. Demand for these commodities is very inelastic in the wide range of prices that are charged. A tax that raises the price paid by the consumer does not greatly reduce the quantity consumed. On the other hand, there are many commodities on which a tax would greatly

reduce consumption and produce little revenue. Examples
of this sort of commodity, where demand is highly elastic,
might be butter, frozen prepared food, tape recordings, and
automobiles priced over $4000.

Another example of the importance of knowing something
of the elasticities of demand is taken from the experience of
Poland under socialism. In countries like Poland income
differentials are quite small. At one price, a given good
may be inaccessible to the vast majority of the population,
but even a small change in price may bring this item within
the range of a low-income worker. Because so many workers have similar incomes, "demand avalanches" have been
observed in the case of such consumer durables as television
sets, radios, and motorcycles. A miscalculation of the elasticity of demand may lead to a severe shortage when a
small price reduction leads to a great increase in demand.

The prices of such basic commodities as cocoa, tin, rubber, and copper have fluctuated over wide ranges—far beyond the prices of the finished products ordinarily sold.

Table 2
World Copper Prices and Production

YEAR	YEARLY AVERAGE PRICE, LONDON (1960 = 100)	WORLD PRODUCTION (1960 = 100)
1960	100	100
1961	93.5	104
1962	95.1	109
1963	95.5	112
1964	143.0	115
1965	190.6	120
1966	225.0	120

SOURCE: *Metal Statistics 1967* (New York: The American Metal Market
Company, 1967). Reprinted with permission.

The supply of these commodities is very inelastic; small changes in demand (a slight shift in the demand schedule) lead to large variations in price. When demand rises, output cannot be expanded quickly. The output of a single copper mine cannot be changed quickly and new mines are not often opened. The supply of copper reaching world markets is therefore less elastic than that of automobiles (see Table 2).

Advertising and the Efficiency of the Economic System

We have assumed thus far that consumers make choices among their opportunities following their preferences, limited by their incomes and guided by the relative prices they have to pay for goods. Many writers have argued that consumer preferences are so heavily guided by advertising that, from a social point of view, choice is arbitrary. (The implication is that with preferences so much subject to manipulation, the economy reaches irrational decisions.) A variety of solutions is offered. Control or elimination of advertising and increased government spending on "public" goods are often advocated. However, much advertising can be regarded as providing useful information to consumers. (For example, the Thursday advertising of the grocery stores allows housewives to plan their shopping in order to take advantage of the sales in different stores.) New products are often more heavily advertised than old products; some persons may argue that consumer choice is better informed because of such advertising. Some important products are not advertised at all—Hershey chocolate bars are not advertised in the United States, and milk is little advertised.

On the other hand, there is heavy advertising of cigarettes, liquor, and soap. The money spent on advertising these products could, it is argued, be spent to better advantage on building schools and housing. Perhaps, but the resources allocated to schools and housing are determined by public consensus; if schools and housing are inadequate, the reason is that the community has failed to vote the necessary appropriations and taxes rather than that advertising has created excessive wants for cigarettes. Would outlays of resources for advertising schools and housing create a community want for these? That advertising cannot manipulate consumer taste without limit is shown by the many unsuccessful attempts to introduce unwanted products: the Edsel car, electric razors (an item that, despite sophisticated advertising, has captured only a small part of the men's razor market), and chlorophyll toothpaste (a fad that was created by advertising and succeeded only for a few months). These few examples of the failures of advertising do not prove that advertising cannot create wants, but they do indicate some qualification to a naïve belief in its omnipotence. Although advertising for such products as liquor, cigarettes, and soap could probably be eliminated without much reduction of consumer knowledge, the assertion that all advertising is of little value to consumers would be inaccurate. The argument is often advanced that advertising contributes to monopoly by reducing the number of sellers of a product. Studies indicate that many of the highly advertised products remain highly competitive in the eyes of their buyers, so that the seller, though he advertises the special virtues of his brand, cannot raise his price above the other brands without losing a large share of the market. Thus the demand for many brands remains highly elastic, and something resembling competition still remains.

Competition and Monopoly

The sketch of how producers and consumers are joined together in carrying out economic decision-making and production has assumed perfect competition—a situation where producers in each industry are so numerous that none can control the output and price of the industry. Where this is true, output will expand or contract to the levels where the price just covers the costs of production.

The formal conditions governing competitive behavior would seem to allow few industries to be called competitive. A firm must be in a position where it is unable to influence price by changing its output; thus there must be a great number of firms in the industry whose customers are able to shift their purchases among these companies. But how many industries fulfill this requirement? If gasoline filling stations were independently owned, there would be enough of them in a city like Chicago to compete effectively with one another. With a high degree of concentration of ownership, filling stations are a better example of *oligopoly* (few sellers) than of competition.

The largest competitive industry is probably agriculture. Surely the conditions governing the production of wheat, oats, and other common grains are competitive; no farmer can influence the price of wheat within the range of the possible variations in his output. There is a highly organized market for wheat—by telephone a farmer can sell carloads for delivery at specified dates at specified places. He can sell to a local grain merchant, who, in turn, can resell the wheat on one of the grain exchanges, or he can sell directly to a processor or larger grain merchant.

The meat-packing industry is an example of an industry that is "workably" competitive. The product is standardized to the extent that many producers offer each grade; there is virtually no branded identity in fresh meat. There were 379 firms slaughtering federally inspected cattle and operating 491 separate plants in the United States in 1962. Almost three-quarters of the cattle slaughtered were produced in the central and mountain states; these states exported cattle to the other regions of the country. There is thus a nationwide market for cattle—no region is self-sufficient or able to exclude the import of beef from other regions. In addition, entry into the slaughtering industry was open; 53 percent of the firms in business in 1962 had entered the industry since 1950. As shown in Table 3, the top ten firms

Table 3
Cattle Slaughter by the Four Largest, Fifth to Tenth Largest, and Ten Largest Firms in the United States, 1950–1962 (Percent)

Firms	1950	1954	1958	1962
1–4	51.5	45.2	35.7	29.5
5–10	8.7	10.0	10.5	10.4
1–10	60.2	55.2	46.2	39.9

SOURCE: Agricultural Economic Report No. 83, *Structural Changes in the Federally Inspected Livestock Slaughter Industry, 1950–62,* U.S. Department of Agriculture, February 1966.

produced 40 percent of the cattle slaughtered in 1962. The decline from 60.2 percent in 1950 suggests that the new firms, employing the most efficient technology, are growing

Table 4
**Share of Federally Inspected Cattle Slaughtered,
by Cumulative Percentage of Firms in the United States,
1950–1962**

Cumulative Percentage of Firms	Cumulative Share of Cattle Slaughtered			
	1950	1954	1958	1962
0	0	0	0	0
10	72	66	62	59
20	81	76	74	72
30	87	84	82	81
40	91	89	88	87
50	95	93	92	92
60	97	96	95	95
70	98	98	97	98
80	100	99	99	99
90		100	100	100
100				

SOURCE: Agricultural Economic Report No. 83, *Structural Changes in the Federally Inspected Livestock Slaughter Industry, 1950–62*, U.S. Department of Agriculture, February 1966.

and prospering with outputs smaller than those of the older, larger firms.

The following excerpts from an article in *The Wall Street Journal* of May 4, 1966 (reprinted with permission), may illustrate how a competitive industry adapts to changes in technology and innovation.

Iowa Beef Packers, Inc. Only 6 Years Old, Gains While Rivals Flounder

"Think money," says D. A. Anderson, president of the company. "That's why I painted everything green."

Be hard-nosed in labor bargaining, work your executives on a six-day week (competitors work five days, Mr. Anderson says, and "then they rationalize the low profit margins with a

golf game"), watch every penny, avoid diversification to con-
centrate entirely on beef. . . . He has built a company that is
only six years old into a flourishing young giant.

In 1964 Iowa Beef . . . already ranked as the nation's 314th
[largest U. S. industrial corporations] plus the third highest
. . . In that year Iowa Beef had the second highest rate of
sales per dollar of invested capital ($20.70) among the 500
[largest U. S. industrial corporations] plus the third highest
profit return on invested capital (31%).

More important, Iowa Beef is making a profitable go in an
industry where some big companies are losing money and other
big companies aren't making much. Many industry leaders turned
long ago to diversification to keep out of the red. . . . In fiscal
1965, Iowa Beef's operating earnings rose 9.8% to a record while
operating net of the nation's nine larger packers dropped 28.5%.

. . . the main reason for Iowa Beef's record . . . is that the
company has developed an efficient mass production system for
buying, processing and distributing that is perfectly fitted to
today's mass marketing of meat through chain stores. . . .
Cattle buyers keep in touch with the company by using two-way
radio equipment in their cars. Because of this, Iowa Beef learns
immediately about cattle purchases and can stop further buying
if capacity has been reached or demand for beef happens to be
low.

To improve and expand its radio system, the company is
completing construction on a $1 million network with 40 towers
capable of giving coverage of parts of six states.

Construction costs are kept down by hiring workers who
eventually will hold jobs in the plants to do much of the construction labor. At its new plant in Dakota City, Neb., just
across the border from Sioux City, Iowa, there were more than
250 such workers, some making $1.25 an hour. . . . Because
the company acts as the prime contractor for its plants, its
building practices haven't led to labor strife.

"With rare exceptions, the people who work for Iowa Beef

aren't the sort who get involved in anything else. . . . They couldn't and work the hours we work."

In the early 1960s, Iowa Beef's stock sold for as low as $3.82, taking into account a subsequent 2-for-1 split in 1963 and a 100% stock dividend in 1965. The stock earlier this year sold for as high as $68.50, but now has tumbled to about $44. . . .

Though the company is a tough bargainer in labor sessions, its wages generally are considered good. The company says the average pay of hourly employees in fiscal 1965 was $8,496 at the Denison plant and $6,897 at the Fort Dodge facility, which was affected by the five-week strike. The industry average is about $6,825. . . . There also is a profit-sharing plan for workers at Denison and a stock-purchase plan for most hourly employees at all plants . . . the average age of the hourly workers at the plant . . . is 28. Raised on or near farms, most are familiar with machinery, says Mr. Walker . . . "and they're used to hard work and don't expect something for nothing."

A leader in automation, Iowa Beef plans further innovations in the cattle and beef industry. This fall, the company hopes to begin breaking up beef carcasses into small meat cuts. . . . Like many other packers, Iowa Beef currently ships only full carcasses to its more than 200 customers . . . [their] new automated breaking facility will save customers the trouble of breaking the carcasses and eliminate some of the middlemen, officials claim.

The company also says the breaking of the carcasses at the packing plant will lower shipping costs by eliminating at least 200 pounds of unwanted fat and bone in the average 750 pound meat carcass before it leaves the packing plant. In addition the company explains that a breaking plant in the Midwest can more efficiently distribute the various cuts of meat throughout the country. For instance, most top sirloins will be shipped to the West . . . while strip steaks, sometimes known as New York cuts, made from other parts of the carcass, usually will be shipped East where they are more commonly eaten.

. . .

This illustration not only gives some idea of what a competitive industry looks like to one of its member firms but implies what adjustments must take place in the industry, as a result of the entry of a successful innovator, that will soon be copied by others. Older firms, operating plants that are no longer as efficient as the newly built plants, have already been forced to close their facilities. Others have remodeled or constructed new plants approaching Iowa Beef's in efficiency.

Where there is competition, the "automatic" adjustment of supply, in the long run, to the level of demand assures an allocation of resources of optimal productivity. But where there is monopoly, resources are not so efficiently allocated. The monopolist can affect the price consumers pay merely by withholding output from the market and creating scarcity of the product. A monopolist will always gain by raising the price of a product above the competitive level. This price increase misallocates resources in the economy; consumers are willing to pay more for a commodity than the "social costs" of the resources. The economic rationale of antitrust action by the government is that such action reduces the power of one firm or a few firms to control prices and output.

Although outright monopoly, where it is not created by legislation or by the ruling of the Federal Communications Commission, the Civil Aeronautics Board, the Patent Office, or other public licensing and regulatory agencies, is very rare in the contemporary economy, concentration of production in a few firms (oligopoly) is not uncommon. The situation where a high percentage of total sales is concentrated in a few firms within an industry is observable in grocery retailing, and in automobile, steel, aluminum, chemical, and electrical equipment manufacturing industries. Prices may be high or low in relation to costs, depending on the sense of discipline and cooperation among the rival firms. There may be a *price leader*, as in cigarettes (and, to some extent, in steel and automobiles), where something approaching monopoly prices will be established by the dominant firm, which knows that the others will follow its lead.

Other products, though not concentrated in a few firms, are produced by a larger number of firms that advertise heavily in an attempt to create an impression among consumers that unique quality exists in their products in comparison with similar products. Prices of these "differentiated" products frequently are almost as sensitive to one another as prices of highly competitive products, even though each product, having a special brand name, would seem to be unique and monopolized by its particular manufacturer.

The degree of concentration of production in the hands of few firms may not indicate monopoly *power*, however, in either the short or the long run. Products of other industries may keep demand extremely elastic for products of highly monopolized industries. Thus steel, aluminum, concrete, and glass "compete" with one another in construction; copper and aluminum compete in the production of electrical conductors; railroads and trucks compete in transportation; the telephone, the mail, and the telegraph compete in communications; and newspapers and television compete in advertising.

Some economic problems arise from departures from competition—either where an industry, for the sake of efficiency, *should* be monopolized (as in the case of a public utility) or where, by merger, patent advantage, or other device, a single firm produces all the output in an industry that might otherwise have several firms. There are few monopolies; there are, however, many industries with few firms.

CHAPTER IV

Distribution and
the Economics of Labor

If all labor were of one kind, if land and capital were similarly of one kind, and if individuals earned their incomes either as laborers, landlords, or lenders, an analysis that showed what determined the level of wages, rent, and interest would also show how incomes are distributed among individuals. But if (as in the real world) labor is not homogeneous and some people earn their incomes partly from labor, partly from interest on investments, and partly from rent, there is no perfect way of inferring income distribution from occupational earnings. Yet we shall discuss primarily the determination of occupational earnings in this chapter.

Relationship of Wages, Productivity, and Demand

It will pay employers to hire extra workers as long as the value of the extra production exceeds the extra wages that must be paid. The extra production that can be obtained by hiring an additional worker is a function of the productivity of that worker; his productivity is affected by the intensity with which he works, by the amount and productivity of the tools he uses, and by the amount of capital and land available. The more capital (in the form of machinery and tools) and land, the greater the productivity of each worker. Even the early nineteenth-century economists understood these relations rather well. Wages would rise as the amount of land and capital per worker rose or as technology improved. Wages would fall as population rose relative to land and capital.

Marx and others argued that, in the conditions of the nineteenth century, the effect of the accumulation of capital and the improvement of technology would be to reduce wages. Marx argued that capitalists would invest in larger and larger factories and would employ machinery that saved labor. The extra demand for labor from the extra factories would not offset the reduction in demand for labor from the "automation" of production. Further, the great increase in output would exceed the capacity of consumer demand to purchase this output. The result of this process, over several years or decades, would be increasing unemployment caused by insufficient demand and rising (automated) supply. Increasing unemployment would lower wages because those out of work would compete for the available jobs by bidding down wages. A cycle of lower demand would be aggravated by the reduced purchases of the laboring class; fewer workers being paid lower wages would lead to a still lower employment level.

If full employment could be maintained through a stimulation of demand, either through government spending or through government monetary policy,[1] these Marxian

Table 5
**Real Industrial Wages in the United Kingdom
and the United States, 1850–1930**

Year	U.K.	U.S.
	1860 = 103	
1850	100	—
1860	103	103
1870	118	93
1880	134	109
1890	166	150
1900	183	170
1910	174	189
1924	197	218
1930	216	240

SOURCES: For United Kingdom, B. R. Mitchell and P. Deane, *Abstract of British Historical Statistics* (New York: Cambridge University Press, 1962). For the United States, *Historical Statistics of the United States, 1789–1945* (Washington, D.C.: Department of Commerce, 1949); Albert Rees, *Real Wages in Manufacturing 1890–1914* (Princeton, N.J.: Princeton University Press, 1961); Clarence Long, *Wages and Earnings in the United States, 1860–1890* (Princeton, N.J.: Princeton University Press, 1960).

predictions would not come to pass; the fully employed working class would benefit from automation because wages would be higher and prices would be lower.

In fact, as shown in Table 5, real wages rose during the last hundred years; real *earnings* rose slower than real

[1] See Chapter V for a discussion of measures to ensure full employment.

wages, owing to a decline in the average hours worked per week in manufacturing—from 60 in 1890 to approximately 47 in 1945. The comparable length of the work week in 1860 may well have been 66 hours. The steady automation of work that has taken place in the past hundred years has greatly raised wages in spite of the theoretical possibility that aggregate demand, under certain conditions, might not have maintained full employment and raised wages.

Emergence of Unionism

The layman's answer to the question of how wages did in fact rise is often that trade unions arose and secured increases in wages through bargaining with employers. Without unions, it is said, wages would have fallen. Yet in 1897 only 2.75 percent of the nonagricultural work force belonged to unions; real wages do not seem to have risen faster since the existence of unions than before unions were an important force. The powerful and steady tendency of wages to rise must therefore be explained by the improvement in technology, accumulation of capital, and improvement in worker skills. Nevertheless, common sense prompts one to ask how "competition" can drive up wages when each worker obviously is at a considerable bargaining disadvantage to his employer. Again, common sense is not always correct, as Galileo is said to have realized when he declared: *Eppur si muove,* "It moves just the same." The wage market resembles other markets in complexity; the equilibrium price that emerges from the millions of transactions in the market is out of the control of any of the participants and rises rather predictably in spite of the absence of any policy formulated to regulate it.

What then has been the economic impact of unions? Surely economic theory confirms that monopolists can raise prices above competitive levels, and unions are, by their nature, monopolies. A group of workers, either with a common craft (like electricians) or with a common employer or industry (like the automobile workers) achieves recognition through election as the sole bargaining agent of the employees. Negotiations are conducted over a contract stipulating wage rates, conditions of work, and fringe benefits including vacations, pensions, and health and disability insurance. When agreement cannot be reached, the union uses its strike weapon to force the employer to either shut down his plant or attempt to operate the plant without the striking union workers. If the union can keep the employer's plant shut down, is the union not in a position to secure a monopoly wage? The answer is yes, up to a point that is determined by the nature of the industry. The effect of higher wages will be to raise the price (shift the supply curve) of the product; if demand for the product is highly elastic, output will decrease and employment of union members will decrease. The greater the percentage of total cost that is composed of wages, the greater will be the shift in the supply curve for any given wage increase. A reasonable conclusion, therefore, is that members of craft unions (typographers, electricians, and airline pilots) have better economic possibilities of raising wages than garment workers, automobile workers, or textile workers. The technological possibilities are limited also—mechanical cotton pickers and automatic elevators set limits on the wages that can be demanded by workers in these industries if the workers are not to eliminate the jobs they are bargaining for. From this analysis even powerful unions can be seen to operate with limitations on wage advancement.

Although improving technology, capital formation, and full employment have raised wages and incomes, poverty has not been eliminated. Ways must be found to improve the functioning of the economic system in order to raise the earnings of those in the lower income brackets and bring into employment either those who are presently unemployable or those who could be trained for useful work. Workers in economically backward regions and in declining and depressed industries could best be helped to find higher incomes through relocation and retraining. The capital and land possessed by Southern rural sharecroppers are insufficient to enable them to practice efficient farming methods, utilizing modern technology. Migration to better-paying jobs in industrial centers probably would be the best adjustment, but the problems of urban living often prevent a rapid, easy adjustment for those whose schooling in the South was only rudimentary and who lack training in mechanical skills. Many workers find themselves with infrequent employment in the depressed mining towns of eastern Kentucky.

Others are poor because they are disabled or sick. Moreover, households without male heads are often poor, lacking at least one wage earner. Improvement of the labor market will not solve this kind of poverty; nor will poverty among the old and retired be cured by changes in opportunities for work.

Some poverty may obtain even where workers are employed but where the jobs pay a very low wage. Here higher wages will lead to higher incomes, but in all probability the higher wages will lead to elimination of the jobs. (For example, when a minimum wage is legislated, employers usually will reduce employment of the lowest-paid workers. Some workers who were formerly employable will be thrown on public welfare for support.) Unionization and minimum-wage legislation are likely to hurt a significant number of workers whose wages are at the bottom of the scale. For these workers, higher incomes will come either through a public supplement to their earnings, if they hold down jobs, or through training programs that raise their productivity.

The Ethics of Wages

We have been describing a rather abstract model of the real world, in which free agents make contracts with one another to specialize in the production and exchange of the goods and services they demand. Division of labor extends to management; some sell their labor and others contract to buy it; some save and accumulate capital funds and others choose not to. If all started with a "tolerable" equality of opportunity and capacity, a system that gave rewards in proportion to the valuations of the market would be ethically defensible. Both labor and capital would be paid according to their productivity. Differentials in earnings would reflect the various advantages and disadvantages of different kinds of employment—the most hazardous and difficult jobs would pay wages high enough to attract workers to undertake them. Differences in income would reflect choices about how hard people wanted to work, as well as the security and safety and the length and expense of training required for different types of employment.

In the real world, opportunities are not equal. Middle-class children have advantages that carry them through school more easily and farther than children from poorer homes. Efforts to make opportunities more equal are reflected in inheritance taxes, progressive income taxes, and free public education. Perfect equality of opportunity is inconceivable under any system; ambitious and bright parents are likely to breed achieving children.

The degree of equality of opportunity and the measures that could effectively increase it are subjects of considerable debate. But beyond this discussion lies the question: How large a measure of equality of income is desirable for those who are not capable of taking advantage of opportunities because they lack the capacity?[2] Finally there is the question: How much does intervention to bring about equality reduce the efficiency of the economy, either by reducing the rate of growth of income or perhaps, at some point, by reducing the level of income itself?

[2] Richard H. Tawney's *Equality* (New York: Macmillan, 1952) provides an eloquent argument for equalizing income rather than merely equalizing opportunity.

CHAPTER V

Aggregate Demand and the Monetary System

In the previous chapters we assumed that the resources of the economy were fully employed, and we discussed how the amount of resources devoted to the production of each product is determined. An increase in the demand for one product leads to a rise in price, thus rationing the limited supply among the consumers. A rise in price attracts additional production from firms already in the industry and, in the longer run, attracts new firms, drawing resources away from other industries whose products are less in demand than the product whose price has risen. The total output does not change; only its composition is determined by the interaction of demand and supply. We must now ask: What determines the total output and what are the forces that cause the output to change? This is explained by the theory of employment, income, and the price level.

In the process of production—the circular flow of income discussed in Chapter II—each productive agent draws a money income from the sale of some service, labor, or capital that he "rents" to employers, and he spends this income for the products or services that he desires to consume, perhaps saving a part of it. In order for there to be demand enough to keep all the productive factors employed, there must be demand enough for the goods that these factors produce. If the economy were being directed from a central planning office the problem would seem quite simple. If we knew the size of the labor force desiring work, we could make certain that the aggregate production plans of the factories included a demand for the required number of workers. We could send out instructions to the factories to include enough workers. If the aggregate demand was not large enough to take off the market all that this "full employment" work force produced, the state could afford either to stockpile the excess production or reduce its price enough to ensure its sale.

In a socialized economy, when unemployment appears, it will be called a mistake of planning, because planning includes forecasting the size of the work force and ordering enough employing units to expand their demands for workers. In a market economy, however, the demand for labor is not looked after in this way. When there is unemployment, a central agency does not issue instructions to employers to take on a certain number of extra workers. Each employer makes a separate judgment about the optimal number of workers and hires additional workers only if "it pays"—only if there is sufficient demand to justify the additional wage expense that will be met by the extra revenue brought in by the extra production. This procedure ensures that workers will be utilized in the most efficient manner, but does it ensure that they will always be employed? What is the mechanism by which a market economy keeps its resources fully employed—that is, keeps the flow of income balanced between consumers, employers, and employees at a level that will provide full employment?

Aggregate demand is analyzed in two closely related ways: by looking at the supplies and demands for goods and services and by looking at the monetary system in which the demands are made. The first method is associated with John Maynard Keynes; the second method is the older approach of monetary theory. The first method traces the clockwise broken line of Figure 1; the second traces the solid counterclockwise line.

The Income-Spending Approach

Let us consider the forces that give rise to demand for output. Spending arises from demand for consumption goods and investment goods.[1] To determine the aggregate demand we must know what determines the consumption and investment demands. Suppose consumption demand always is a fixed percentage of consumers' income. Consumption is thus not an independent determinant of income. But what determines the amount of investment demand? We could mention many factors: expectations about the profit-

---

[1] Figure 5 sets out the data of the composition of the gross national product in the United States in 1964. It is particularly helpful in showing how saving and government spending and taxing affect the circular flow of income pictured more simply in Figure 1. Both figures omit the effects of exports and imports.

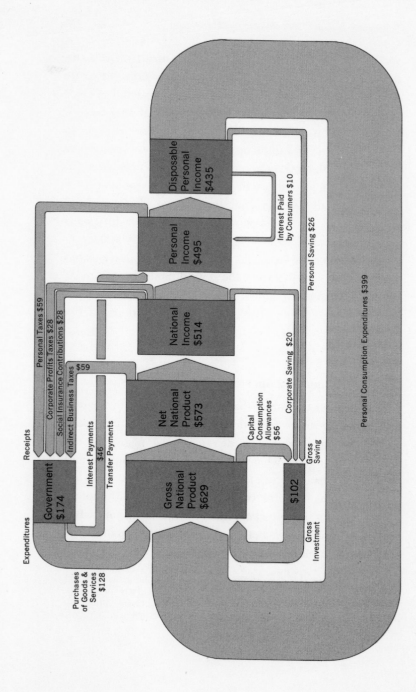

Figure 5

The Flow of Income and Expenditures in the United States, 1964 (Billions of Dollars)

ability of business in the future, the rate of interest, the present level of demand, and so on. Keynes argued that the level of investment demand is rather arbitrary and is determined independently of the variables we are discussing. If consumption plus investment determines the level of income, but consumption is itself determined by income, the conclusion must follow that the level of income is in fact

---

NCTE: Explanation of the flow for Figure 5 on facing page.

The gross national product (the final market value of the nation's total annual output of goods and services) amounted to $629 billion in 1964, which is the sum of personal consumption expenditures ($399 billion), government purchases of goods and services ($128 billion), and gross investment ($102 billion).

When capital consumption (the value of machinery and plant used up in production), which amounts to $56 billion, is deducted, the net national product of $573 billion remains.

After deduction of indirect business taxes (including miscellaneous adjustments) totaling $59 billion, which flows to the government sector, national income—$514 billion—remains.

From national income, social insurance contributions ($28 billion) and corporate profits taxes ($28 billion) go to the government sector, while corporate saving (undistributed profits of $20 billion) flows into gross saving.

To the remaining $438 billion is added $46 billion in transfer and interest payments from the government plus interest of $10 billion paid by consumers. Personal income thus totals $494 billion.

From personal income, individuals paid personal taxes of $59 billion to government. This leaves $435 billion as disposable personal income.

Disposable personal income flows into three main channels:

Personal consumption expenditures	$399 billion
Personal saving	26 billion
Interest paid by consumers	10 billion

Personal saving, corporate saving, and capital consumption amount to $102 billion in gross saving, equivalent (after adjustment for minor items) to gross investment. (Slight discrepancies in totals are due to rounding.)

determined by the level of investment demand. Each increment of investment will give rise to additional demand that creates additional income that creates a proportionate addition to consumption demand. The equilibrium level of income is the level that generates enough consumption so that consumption plus investment equals the given level of income. This approach suggests that fluctuations in employment and output are caused by fluctuations in investment demand and that consumption follows changes in income but does not lead these changes. The theory was also used to suggest the difficulty of stabilizing investment at a level high enough to ensure full employment, if the government can, at most, influence only the rate of interest (that is, the price borrowers must pay for the funds they invest). The conclusion was therefore that a new and independent source of demand for goods must be found to ensure that the aggregate demand would be large enough to employ the labor force fully; this independent source of demand was government expenditures. If government spending were changed to fill the gap, aggregate demand could always be kept at the full-employment level.

The Keynesian picture of the economy was formulated at the depth of a severe depression. Investment had shrunk to a very low level; consumption had fallen; one-fourth of the working force was unemployed; there did not seem to be any means by which investors or consumers, by themselves, could raise demand to generate higher income and employment. Only the government had the ability to stimulate demand by spending more. But in a situation not so hopelessly trapped, are there no forces through which the private sector can stabilize itself? We must look at each component of demand.

1. Consumption. Suppose consumption is related not merely to this year's income but to the income level that consumers have come to expect from their past experience. When one year's income falls, consumers will go on spending at their accustomed level, drawing for a while on past savings. Thus the current level of consumption may rise above the current level of personal income for a short time.

2. Investment. Suppose aggregate demand falls and employment and income are lower than before. Investment will not be as attractive to businessmen as before, because there is already idle productive capacity. The demand for investment will therefore be lower; interest rates are likely to fall in response to the lower demand for investment. At lower interest rates, there will be an incentive to invest more, but interest rates might not fall enough to stimulate a volume of added investment sufficiently large to compensate for the gap created by the initial reduction in demand.

In the event that the price mechanism failed to keep aggregate supply and demand equal at full employment, the Keynesian analysis pointed to the government's use of fiscal policy to fill the gap. This policy can be applied by allowing either expenditures or revenues to move up and down to compensate for the private movements. The result is either a budget deficit or (to combat inflation) a budget surplus. The Keynesian view was that private demand is not sufficient to maintain full employment and that government should generate whatever extra demand is needed. In practice, the attempt to use the American federal budget as a "countercyclical" force has been difficult, owing to the difficulty in securing congressional approval of large changes in spending and to the long delays in implementing spending proposals.

The Monetary Approach

The other leading approach to a theory of aggregate demand looks at the other side of the circular flow of income. Where the Keynesian theory concentrates on the supply and demand for goods and services, the older monetary theory analyzes the flows of money that occur in the process. The two approaches ought to give the same answers because both are concerned with aspects of the same reality. However, their differences are not harder to understand than the different weather predictions we would get by looking at barometric pressure, wind velocity, and wind direction. The two approaches are parts of the reality we are studying; they do not always predict consistently.

The monetary approach attempts to explain the level of employment and prices by looking at the stock of money being held by consumers and firms. The Keynesian theory is built around the stable relation between consumption and income. The monetary theory is built around the stable relation between cash holdings of the public and income. In 1960, about seven months' income was held as money by individuals and business firms. (Money is here defined as currency, demand deposits—that is, checking accounts—and savings deposits.) The monetary theory holds that the amount of money people seek to hold is not arbitrary but is determined by the utility of the services money provides and represents a reserve of purchasing power held to even out the uncertain and irregular timing of the receipt of income and expenditures for goods and services. At any time, if the community finds itself retaining more than seven months' income as money, people will attempt to reduce their holdings of money. But the community as a whole cannot reduce its stock of money; as a dollar passes from one person to the next, the total number of dollars does not change. What the community can affect is the price level (assuming there is full employment)—as everyone tries to reduce his money balances, demand for goods will rise and, because aggregate supply cannot change when there is full employment, prices will rise. The community, in making decisions about the size of its money stock, indirectly determines the price level.

Suppose the money stock is under the control of the government. Is it not possible, by controlling the size of the money stock, to control aggregate demand and the price level? When the quantity of money is kept stable (managed roughly so as to increase at the rate of growth of the gross national product), there will be no instability of demand. The key to stable employment, it is argued, is stable management of the money supply.[2]

The two approaches to explaining aggregate demand are interrelated. In the Keynesian approach, investment is affected by the rate of interest. However, a change in the quantity of money also affects the rate of interest and the ability of banks to make new loans. Therefore the effect on aggregate demand that is attributed by monetary theory to changes in the money supply is explained by Keynesian theory as a change in investment demand.

Both theories explain the effect of a government budget deficit in a time of full employment in a similar way. In the

[2] See Milton Friedman, *Capitalism and Freedom* (Chicago: University of Chicago Press, 1963), chap. iii.

one approach, a budget deficit affects prices because it reflects a demand for output in excess of what the economy is capable of producing. The excess leads to inflation. In the other approach, a budget deficit will be paid for by an increase in the quantity of money—the government will either print new dollars to be used in the banking system or sell its bonds to banks, a process that will increase the deposit balances in the accounts of the Treasury. The Treasury will spend the dollars that have been newly created, either on the printing press or in the banks, for purchasing goods and services from the private sector. This increase of money in the hands of the public will lead to increased demand for output and an inflation similar to that explained by the Keynesian theory.

The Banking System and the Money Supply

The stock of money consists of coin and currency issued by the federal government and bank deposits that are used by individuals for making payments by check. To be realistic, to the definition of the stock of money we might add traveler's checks (which are almost as acceptable as currency and often are more acceptable than checks) and credit cards. But then we should include government savings bonds and other assets that are not used as a medium of exchange but can quickly be sold for money. With such a range of money, money substitutes, and reserves, a definition of money will have to make arbitrary distinctions, and we will call money what most people regard as money—currency, coin, and bank demand (checking) and time (savings) deposits. Of the total money stock defined in this way ($396 billion in May 1967),[3] one-third was demand deposits and almost three-fifths was time deposits. Demand deposits accounted for over three times the amount included in currency and coin. Therefore the money supply is largely bank money, and management of the money supply requires management of banks.

A commercial bank accepts deposits from individuals. Suppose $100 of currency is deposited in a bank. The bank makes a bookkeeping entry, giving the customer the right to withdraw up to $100 or to write checks to others for this amount. But if a good deal of the $100 is left in the bank most of the time, the bank will have more currency than it needs to keep on hand for meeting the demands of its customers. The profitability of banks arose from their discovery that they could lend out some of this cash reserve. Commercial banks thus hold "fractional reserves," in that they do not have more than about 16 percent of their liabilities to their deposit customers available in cash at any time. If all customers would attempt to withdraw their deposits, banks would immediately be insolvent (bankrupt).

The bank must compromise its motive to maximize profits (lend all its reserves) with its motive of prudence in keeping a reserve adequate to meet demands that are made on it. Banks are supervised by various government authorities to ensure that they keep what is regarded as "prudent" cash reserves (including the deposit balances that banks themselves hold with Federal Reserve banks) and assets (primarily short-term government bonds called Treasury bills) that can be sold quickly for cash.

With a new source of cash, a bank finds itself with re-

[3] *Federal Reserve Bulletin,* June 1967.

serves in excess of its requirements. The excess will be loaned to a customer, for whom a new bookkeeping entry of a deposit account is created. This expansion of loans is related to demand for investment, because one way of financing investment is to borrow from banks. The rate of investment can therefore be influenced by regulation of the expansion of bank loans. The expansion of bank loans is regulated by the rate of expansion of bank reserves. But the expansion of bank reserves can come about only through (1) the public taking cash it had been carrying around and depositing this cash in the banks, or (2) the printing of more currency either by the Treasury or by the Federal Reserve System. The Treasury can create more currency by printing money to pay for a budget deficit. But in practice, the Treasury sells government bonds to the Federal Reserve System and receives a deposit account in a Federal Reserve Bank. When the Treasury writes checks on the account to pay for the goods purchased from private individuals by the government, the balances are transferred from the account of the Treasury to the private commercial banks in which the individuals keep their own checking accounts. In this way, the reserves of the private banking system are increased by the deficit spending of the Treasury. The purchase of a new government bond by the Federal Reserve System adds to the purchase of the banking system in the same way as would the printing of a new dollar bill. The banks can use these newly created reserves as a base on which to expand their loans to their customers, up to the minimum ratio required by the Federal Reserve System.

The Federal Reserve System has the power to control the reserves of the banking system through its own purchases and sales of government bonds and by lending reserves directly to the private commercial banks. If it chooses, the Federal Reserve Bank can sell a bond to an insurance company, bank, or other private investor. When the bond is paid for with a check, the Federal Reserve Bank that sold the bond will deduct the amount kept on deposit with it by the purchaser's bank. Thus an "open-market" sale of government bonds can be used to reduce (or increase) the level of reserves available to the banking system. Through its open-market intervention, the Federal Reserve System can regulate the growth of the money supply, the interest rate, and the level of current investment. Through its influence on these, the Federal Reserve System can influence the level of prices and employment. The subject of current debate is not whether the Federal Reserve System can influence prices and employment but how accurately it can handle the "fine-tuning" of the economy.

CHAPTER VI

International Trade

The preceding analysis has assumed that there was no foreign trade and that all production and consumption took place within a *closed system*. In fact, United States imports are roughly 4 percent of the national income—a low level of international trade, but by no means so insignificant that the relationship of the domestic economy to the international economy can be ignored.

International trade benefits a country in the same way as domestic trade does: it permits the exchange of our products for the products of those who can produce them more cheaply than we. The division of labor that permits greater efficiency lowers the costs of production and gives rise to exchange. Division of labor need not be merely within national frontiers; Dutch cheeses and tulips, Danish furniture,

Swiss watches, Saudi Arabian oil, Bolivian tin, Japanese radios, and British woolens are familiar to all readers, just as California wine and oranges, Kentucky bourbon, Southern textiles, and Detroit automobiles are examples of the degree of regional specialization within the nation. Division of labor among regions can be explained by differences in climate, soil conditions, and resource endowment, in the same way that cultural differences explain why New York is the center of the women's fashion industry, Providence the center of the costume jewelry industry, Chicago the center of the men's clothing industry, and Nashville the center of popular music recording.

Domestic Adjustment to Economic Change

The problems that arise in international trade are similar to those that arise in regions of the domestic economy— Appalachia, the rural South, and industrial New England. The migration of the textile industry from New England left depressed areas; the isolation of Appalachia and the progress in the rest of the country left a wide income gap between the two areas. Adjustment within the American economy to economic changes is sometimes slow and painful. The mechanization of Southern agriculture and the prosperity of the industrial North forced workers from the South and drew them to the North, a desirable adjustment to maintain employment and raise incomes. But the adjustment has not been painless. The migration of labor and capital and the retraining of workers accomplish adjustment to change between regions within the economy. But migration of labor and capital is more difficult (though not uncommon) between different countries. In the nineteenth century, there were large intercountry transfers of population and capital that helped to speed adjustment. But language and immigration barriers make transfers of population between countries more difficult than transfers within a country, and although there are often fewer restrictions against international investment, this type of investment is seldom as easy to accomplish as domestic investment. In these respects, the problems of adjustment in international trade are similar to, although more difficult than, adjustment problems in domestic trade. Added to these problems is the frequency of domestic policies that impede adjustment to division of labor; in the interests of national defense or national prestige, certain kinds of industrial activity are often demanded. An automobile industry, a steel industry, and an airline are the most fashionable choices at the present time—every self-respecting developing country insists on having some of these fashionable industries.

PROTECTIONISM VERSUS FREE TRADE

Suppose Iowa decided that its welfare required that automobiles be manufactured within the state. Because the United States Constitution forbids a state from obstructing or taxing the importation or exportation of goods, Iowa cannot impose a tariff barrier that would give protection to its automobile manufacturers, and Iowa therefore would have to subsidize its automobile manufacturers. But suppose Iowa, like a national state, could impose tariffs on imports; the results are not difficult to predict. Automobiles in Iowa would be much more expensive than before protection; capital and labor in Iowa would be diverted to the production of a commodity that could be obtained more cheaply through the export of corn to another state. Why then would a nation engage in protection when such a policy would be unwise for a region to undertake? Adam Smith justified protection of industries essential to the nation's defense—in his day, thought to be Britain's peacetime merchant marine. If in war, a rapid build-up of the nation's navy were needed, the merchant marine provided a reserve of experienced sailors and a large number of ships that could be converted to warships. Perhaps a steel industry and an airplane industry would serve the same function in more recent times. But Smith was under no illusions that the nation would not be paying a price in peacetime for its added security.

A second justification of protection is called the infant industry argument. In a developing country, new firms may lose large sums of money before achieving the level of skill and efficiency needed to compete with established foreign firms. Lacking such large capital resources and the willingness to take great risks, native businessmen will be unwilling to undertake new, though in the long run often profitable, enterprises. The state can intervene and can either provide a subsidy to the new enterprise or levy a tariff (tax) on the importation of the good from abroad. The higher price that can be charged by the domestic producer will then subsidize his entry into the infant industry. But what happens to the infant when it grows up? The argument that justifies a tariff subsidy requires that such subsidy be removed in the future. In practice this procedure has been difficult, and many infant industries have been established that could not compete without a continuation of the subsidies. Tariffs, in these cases, interfere with the long-run international division of labor and reduce national and international real income.

INTERNATIONAL CUSTOMS UNIONS

In an intermediate position between protection and free trade, international customs unions have been developed as free trade areas. Trade among the member countries is unrestricted; trade between a member country and the rest of the world is subject to the tariff schedule agreed upon in common. To the extent that a customs union lowers (with respect to the rest of the world) the average tariffs of the countries that enter it, the customs union is a step toward the greater international division of labor. But if the tariffs are raised to the levels of the member whose policies were previously highly restrictive, the customs union will reduce international specialization in all countries. An area with free trade within and tariffs on trade with nations outside may divert trade away from those countries outside the customs union whose exports are cheaper than those of countries inside the customs union. Such partial movements toward free trade involve gains and losses that correspond to the increase and decline of international division of labor they bring about.

International Adjustments to Economic Change

The adjustments that change the degree of international specialization are sometimes dramatic but usually are seldom in the public notice. In the 1870s Denmark very rapidly changed from a wheat exporter to an exporter of dairy products and pork under the impact of competition from wheat grown on the American Great Plains. Hong

Kong and Japan have entered the world markets for many products, most recently with textiles, watches, cameras, and electronic equipment. These changes require resource adjustments in many countries as some industries expand and others contract in the face of competition.

What we are more likely to notice in international trade are the problems of the payments mechanism that arise in the process of adjusting the international division of labor and the domestic allocation of resources.

The adjustments that take place among regions within one nation do not lead to payments crises. Suppose people in Iowa shift their purchases from pork to shrimp. They will be transferring payment to other states through checks drawn on their bank in Iowa. Because initially Iowa will not be exporting more to other states, banks in Iowa will find themselves with a deficit in their balance of payments with the rest of the country. Each bank will contract its loans or investments enough to maintain its own liquidity, and each will be losing its reserves—in this case its deposits with Federal Reserve banks and with correspondent banks in New York and Chicago. Eventually the contraction of credit in Iowa, coupled with the reduction of sales of pork, will help cut back imports of shrimp and other products to the level that can be afforded by the export of pork (and other products). With a shift in preferences toward shrimp, the probability is that Iowa's total exports and imports will be permanently higher. Within the United States, the payments mechanism functions well enough so that we are not aware of the special problem of balancing payments between regions of the country. Why then are there payments problems in international trade?

When Iowa's payments are in deficit, Iowa's banks will

have to sell assets for money in order to remain solvent. Within the country, a bank can easily sell government bonds or borrow from the Federal Reserve banks. The existence of both a central bank and a nationwide market in financial assets means that an Iowa bank can manage its reserves more easily than can an independent nation.

A second distinction between Iowa and a sovereign nation is that the adjustment in Iowa might lead to a migration of labor from Iowa. The contraction of credit in Iowa would reduce demand, lower Iowa prices, and create either unemployment or lower wages and incomes or both. Wages outside Iowa would be unaffected, and the differential would induce some workers to emigrate. When trade is between nations, emigration is no longer so simple, owing to barriers of language and culture and restrictions on immigration.

Suppose, after a period of balance in foreign payments, imports to the United States increase. What is the effect? Foreigners will be accumulating bank balances in dollars in the amount of the new surplus of imports over exports. Foreigners will not wish to hold the additional balances of dollars and therefore will sell them to their central banks. If the foreign central banks do not wish to accumulate dollar reserves, they will offer these reserves for sale in a market where buyers and sellers are trading in money balances. If the market were perfectly free, the price of dollars in foreign money would fluctuate and, in this example, depreciate. Whereas before, $2.50 bought one English pound, $2.75 is now required to do so. The effect of such a change in the exchange rate is to raise the dollar prices of imported goods. With imports more expensive, consumers will have an incentive to turn to domestically produced goods. At the same time, the lower exchange rate will raise the dollar prices of our exports, giving us an incentive to export more. These two effects will operate to reduce the deficit in our payments and restore their balance.

However, at the present time, the exchange markets are not free to fluctuate with supply and demand. Instead our central bank stands committed to buy or sell gold to other central banks at $35.00 per ounce. The effect of this commitment is that when the exchange rate depreciates, an ounce of gold, bought for $35.00 per ounce, will buy more British pounds when shipped to England than $35.00 spent to buy foreign exchange in the market. The effect of the government's buying and selling policy is to prevent the foreign-exchange rate from fluctuating outside a very narrow range. With the foreign-exchange rate pegged in this way, how do our payments adjust themselves into balance, once an imbalance develops? Unless the Federal Reserve Bank decides to contract the reserves of the member banks, the loss of gold to foreigners need not cause any domestic contraction. We can continue importing more than we export as long as our gold stock lasts or as long as foreign central banks are willing to accumulate dollar balances. Even when a country is running out of gold, the central banks of other countries have occasionally loaned their gold reserves as a means of stretching the gold reserves of the deficit country. All of these measures allow a country to postpone adjustment to a deficit in its balance of payments.

International balance would be easier to maintain if central banks were not responsible for domestic policies that often conflict with international balance. Balance could be restored internationally if, in a time of deficit, the money supply at home were contracted. If domestic monetary and fiscal policy is expansionary, it will conflict with international policy. In the past some ingenious compromises have been tried but none has worked well. Our payments problems will be temporarily easier if we induce foreigners to hold dollar balances. We can do this if interest rates in our country are kept high relative to the rest of the world. But high interest rates discourage domestic investment and slow down the rate of growth; moreover, they may lead to unemployment. Therefore a feasible program might be to enforce a tight money policy to attract foreign balances at the same time that we operate under a fiscal deficit to stimulate employment. We can preserve full employment and temporarily preserve an international payments balance but at the cost of a slower rate of economic growth.

The fundamental problem in international trade is to achieve the best allocation of resources in each national economy. Efficient allocation requires specialization, which requires that some resources be devoted to the production of exports in order to finance the imports that can be obtained more cheaply than by domestic production. Exports ultimately imply imports. We often act and talk as if imports made us poorer, either by threatening the nation's balance of payments or by taking away jobs from the domestic work force. An efficient economy finds jobs for its workers but not in industries where production costs are cheaper abroad. The special problems of international trade arise from political differences, from national insistence on promoting industry at the expense of agriculture or certain industries at the expense of others (for example, a steel industry instead of a bicycle industry), from international barriers to mobility of labor and capital, and from the possible conflict between nations with regard to monetary and trade policies.

CHAPTER VII

Some Applications
of Economic Analysis

A few relatively simple applications of economic reasoning will be discussed in this section in order to suggest the use of economics. In general, models of how a market system organizes production and distribution simplify thinking about problems by ensuring that all causes and effects, in their most likely order of magnitude, have been taken into account in predicting the outcome of any given action. A remarkable amount of useful economic analysis centers around the significance of the intersection of demand and supply curves and the consequences of setting prices that depart from the equilibrium level. The first illustration from the Russian experience should make this application clear.

The Problems of "Disequilibrium Prices"

A selection from the weekly British magazine *The Economist* [1] provides a useful guide to an understanding of the
functioning of a price system. The price system is a mechanism for making decisions; consumers are guided by prices
in their selection of what goods to consume and producers
are guided by prices in determining what and how much of
certain products to supply. What happens when the price
system is not employed in making these decisions can be
seen from this selection.

In Russian communist terms the country has plenty to be
proud of, and most of the inconveniences of life can be defended
as necessary evils, to be endured bravely for the sake of achieving a greater good. A significant part of public opinion is probably prepared to accept this view, and the conditions are endured with surprisingly little complaint. Queues are still the
first thing that catch the western visitor's eye: queues waiting
each morning for the shops to open, queues of 100 or 200 people
who have got wind of a consignment of fresh fish, queues for
eggs and scarce kinds of tinned fruit, queues waiting every
evening in the cold outside ice-cream parlours and restaurants,
queues even to buy a quick drink at a wretched windy street
kiosk instead of a warm pub, queues of people standing twenty
minutes in the middle of Moscow before they can get a taxi even
outside the rush hour. . . . The queues do not, of course, mean
that Russians are hungry or that they live in a siege economy.
They are the rough-and-ready means by which a permanent
rationing system is implemented, avoiding the bureaucracy and
the embarrassment of issuing ration cards. Russia is still a

[1] *The Economist*, November 11, 1967, pp. 608–609. Reprinted with
permission.

country with an acute shortage of capital. Consumer goods are scarce because the planners cannot spare enough resources to make them. In a western economy, in similar circumstances, prices would move upwards until demand for the scarce goods was no greater than the supply. The rich could buy without queueing, but the poor would have to do without.

In Russia, prices of the most essential goods stay low, and rich and poor have an equal chance of buying what is scarce; it is simply a matter of getting into the queue in time. Those who come too late inquire when the next consignment will be on sale, and take care to arrive well before the shop opens so as to get near the door. For the planner the system makes excellent sense, because the extra time and trouble imposed on shoppers costs him nothing. For the public, the inconvenience is multiplied by the fact that over 90 percent of women have jobs, which leaves them very little time to shop in any case, and concentrates most of the shopping in a few hours before and after work and during the lunch break.

The lack of things for people to spend their money on creates very distorted demand patterns. . . . It accounts for the workmen who are often to be seen getting comprehensively drunk on vodka, held down by caviar or salmon, in expensive restaurants. This looks marvellously democratic, until one realises that a lot of westerners might also be consuming champagne and caviar if they were unable to put their money into a far better diet at home plus a motor car, nice clothes for the wife, and a house mortgage.

Railroad Rate Setting. The New York Subway System

A subway transit system like New York's does not cover its expenses from its passenger revenues.[2] Subway fares

2 Discussion of the problem is drawn from the study of William S. Vickrey, "Revising New York's Subway Fare Structure," *Journal of*

have not been raised as much as wages and other costs have
risen in the past twenty years. Of the possible solutions to
the problem of covering the deficits of the transit system,
abandoning the system is not acceptable because (1) the
burden thrown on city streets, buses, and automobiles
would raise the costs of transporting the people far more
than would a substantial fare increase, and (2) the fact can
be established that the mass of patrons would continue
using the subway at higher fares, indicating that, compared
with existing alternatives, the subway is preferred to the
available alternatives by the people who use it.

Thus the subway system should be preserved. But should
fares be raised or should the deficits be assumed by the
taxpayers? Let us put aside the question of covering the
deficits through public subsidies. The problem then becomes one of how to secure enough revenue from the passengers themselves. Investigation by Professor William
Vickrey has shown that only at the peak hours of traffic, in

Operations Research Society of America, III (February 1955). Vickrey's statement of optimal resource use follows:

> To achieve optimum utilization in the economist's sense, it is
> necessary to insure that the value of the benefits produced by all
> of the services provided by a utility shall exceed the costs of ren-
> dering that service by as large a margin as possible.
>
> If we are to be assured that this excess, or social gain, is as
> great as possible, service must be provided and used to such a
> degree that no further possible service remains that would carry a
> benefit to the users greater than the increment of costs occasioned
> by the increment of service. Conversely, no service should be ren-
> dered where the costs occasioned exceed the value of the service.
> For example, if there is a train operating between two points at a
> given time on which it can be reliably predicted that there will be
> a substantial number of vacant seats, so that additional passengers
> could be carried at almost negligible cost, and if there are poten-
> tial passengers who would ride this train between the two points if
> the fare were reduced, then the existing fare fails, to this extent,
> to produce an economically efficient utilization of transit facilities.

the morning and evening, is the system used at its capacity —all the equipment and all the employees are needed in service at these hours. During the rest of the day trains are relatively empty. Thus most of the expense of carrying passengers can be attributed to the short period in each day when the system operates at capacity. This is the period when the elasticity of demand by each customer is the lowest, when an increase in charges will lead to the least reduction of traffic, and when any reduction of traffic will permit the greatest reduction in expenses. Thus the study concluded that any increase in fares should fall on passengers traveling during the peak hours and that fares during the remainder of the day should be reduced. The differential pricing would, by itself, encourage passengers to alter their travel habits and redistribute the load on the system in a manner that would reduce expenses. The question of justice to subway travelers thus was avoided; a fare rise was assumed to be acceptable if the net income of the system were thereby increased. After a careful analysis of the elasticities of demand and the nature of costs, Professor Vickrey recommended a reform of the revenue system of New York's subways. Of course, his advice was not taken.

Obsolescence of Machinery

Competition from Hong Kong, Japan, India, and many other exporters of cheap textiles has reduced the demand for British textile production. Consequently, British firms are earning a low return on investment; many firms have shut down altogether. Yet the idle machinery in old plants is sometimes brought back into production at times when demand and prices rise. This procedure limits the earnings of the firms that remain in production. The British government has a program to buy idle spinning machinery from its owners in order to reduce the capacity of the industry, diminish output, and thereby raise the earnings of the remaining firms. At first glance this seems a reasonable policy —the pains of a declining industry can be relieved and shortened (at public expense) if the least efficient firms are eliminated quickly.[3]

The owners of inefficient machinery will keep it in operation or idle as the extra costs of raw material, labor, and other variable expenses equal the extra revenue obtained from selling the product. If these costs exceed the extra revenues, then the firm must choose between holding the plant and machinery idle in anticipation of better times or higher scrap prices and selling the machinery at its scrap value. The government subsidy has the effect of raising the scrap value and thus increasing the number of machines sold for scrap. Accordingly, what benefit is there? The firm that sells its machines is at an advantage—it would have held them idle without the subsidy. But the industry is no stronger—British manufacturers are not better able to sell cheaply to compete with the foreign suppliers. And as long as Britain does export cotton goods, British manufacturers will be no better able to raise their prices in a competitive world market when largely idle machines are scrapped at home, removing an insignificant part of world capacity. This policy would seem to make no sense to the

[3] The British government enacted a law in 1959 that allows the Board of Trade to pay two-thirds of the cost of removing excess capacity and to charge the remaining one-third to the firms remaining in the industry. See S. Rottenberg, "Adjustment to Senility by Induced Contraction," in *Journal of Political Economy,* 72 (December 1964).

industry (that is, the firms that remain in production). Such a policy helps those who eventually will leave, but this help hardly merits a charge on the ordinary British taxpayer.

Agricultural Price Supports. Who Benefits?

Many unintended effects of price supports can be predicted with a small amount of economic theory. Price supports benefit farmers in proportion to the value of supported crops they sell on the market. The poor farmers are largely subsistence farmers and therefore do not derive much, if any, benefit from a price support program. But do all farmers who raise crops for the market benefit? Consider the rapid reduction of the agricultural labor force during the past twenty years. What has determined the rate at which the farm population has been reduced? Because urban wages are little affected by the number of farmers leaving agriculture and because industrial wages have been high enough in the postwar period to attract a steady migration from agriculture, the earnings of agricultural workers clearly would be little affected by changes in farm income (at full employment). Before farm labor could benefit, demand for labor in agriculture would have to rise enough to cancel out the differential of urban wages. The argument is therefore advanced that farm price supports have raised the value of agricultural land and have not altered labor income. Thus the price support program does not benefit the tenant, sharecropper, or farm laborer.[4]

[4] See D. Gale Johnson, "Agricultural Price Policy and International Trade," *Essays in International Finance*, No. 19, June 1954.

The Problems of Indonesia

The greatest problem of all—and the one that President Suharto is most immediately concerned about—is Indonesia's shattered economy—if it can be called an economy.[5] On the books, Indonesia went bankrupt years ago. It owes $2.4 billion to foreign creditors, and its exports bring in nowhere nearly enough money to meet even the interest payments. The country has no foreign currency reserves and almost no foreign credit; the rupiah is literally not worth the paper it is printed on. The cost of living quintupled during the first six months of 1966 and there is little hope of stopping its rise. No one knows how many people are on the government payroll, but the estimates range from fewer than 2 million to more than 5 million—not including the army's 500,000 men. Because for all practical purposes there is no income tax (all payments are voluntary) and because the government receives little revenue of any kind, it is forced to print almost all the money it needs.

FOUR MACHINES, FOUR CREWS

The lack of foreign currency has left Indonesia's industrial plant in a shambles. There is no money to import either the spare parts or the raw materials necessary to keep the country's machines running. Indonesian industry currently runs at 30 percent of normal production.

In accordance with his "nonaligned" stance, former President Sukarno took equipment from any country willing to

[5] Material in this section based on article in *Time*, 88 (July 15, 1966). Courtesy *Time*, The Weekly Newsmagazine; copyright Time Inc. 1966.

lend him the money to pay for it. Consequently, the electricity plant at Makasar, for example, operates by means of generators from four different countries, with the result that one machine cannot be cannibalized to supply spare parts for the others. Furthermore, the services of four separate groups of maintenance men are required.

In the countryside, where 80 percent of the population still lives, the ravages of the world's worst chronic inflation are scarcely felt. Most families can grow enough food to get along and often have enough left over to barter for clothes and even bicycles. In the cities, life for most is not so easy. The monthly wage of an average white-collar worker would barely buy a round of drinks in the Hotel Indonesia bar. To make ends meet, city dwellers have invented a sort of guerrilla economy. Almost everyone has a racket.

RICE FOR TEACHER

Civil servants appear at the office only long enough to sign in and spend most of the day doing other jobs, such as driving taxis or peddling their influence. Clerks and secretaries cart away office supplies to sell on the black market. Chauffeurs and bus drivers put in extra hours hauling passengers and pick up extra pocket money by siphoning gasoline from their tanks and selling it. Soldiers set up roadblocks to exact a few rupiahs from every passing vehicle. Schools are supposedly free, but teachers expect donations of money or rice from their students. At ports, longshoremen and police openly loot incoming cargoes; one favorite ploy is to remove the vital parts of imported machinery and sell them back to their desperate owners shortly after delivery.

The result is unbounded chaos. Ports are hopelessly clogged, government services are all but paralyzed, and business is wildly inefficient. A visiting American economist recently warned that the time may soon arrive "when a person spends all his time and energy going from one job to another, so that he gets almost nothing done on any of them."

The examples of economic problems discussed above will give some indication of the uses of economic analysis. The dislocations caused by inflation are evident, even when they are somewhat concealed, as exemplified by attempts to prevent the proper allocation of resources (queueing in Russia) and to prevent banks from utilizing all of their savings (reserve requirements). The workings of the simple notions of supply and demand are demonstrated by the subway fare study and by the case of the British subsidy causing the scrapping of machinery. The present structure of subway fares encourages people to utilize the subway system when its extra costs are a maximum. Another structure of pricing would encourage travel at more economical hours—perhaps even reducing the total amount of travel. The price system in the British example failed to provide the result that was expected. Similarly the farm subsidy program often benefits a group of people that probably does not need public help (those who own agricultural land) but does not help those whose incomes are low enough to merit public support. Sufficient numbers of people were ignorant or were adequately deceived to permit adoption of these policies. Economists win the debates but politicians win the elections.

CHAPTER VIII

Economics and Social Reform

Questions Left Unanswered by Economic Theory

Economic theory does not tell us much about the "good society." The ancient Greek ideal was a body of free citizens supported by an agrarian economy that was worked by slaves. It was an economy of free enterprise and private property but one that utilized a high level of taxation for public works and for the support of religious observances in common. The person whose activities were directed to the accumulation of wealth was not thought worthy of citizenship in the free society of Athenians.

Nineteenth- and twentieth-century Western economies saw the development of industry, the relative decline of agriculture, and the organization of the free-enterprise system by entrepreneurs who owned their companies. As the scale of manufacturing grew, the public corporation, where the owners were shareholders who did not participate in the management of the company, became the more typical enterprise. Many writers have pointed to this important trend as the separation of ownership from management and have concluded that (1) management of large corporations is indifferent to the rate of return to the absentee shareholders (Adam Smith); (2) management is headed by financial experts whose interests conflict with the interests of engineers (production for profit instead of for use— Thorstein Veblen); (3) the corporation becomes bureaucratized in the hands of professional managers and is ready for socialism, a system in which ownership passes from the absentee capitalist shareholders to an absentee public (Joseph Schumpeter and, to a degree, J. K. Galbraith). The huge corporation, deplored by many as a monster and a threat to competition in each industry (Henry C. Simons and A. Smith) is welcomed by others as the engine of our prosperity (Galbraith).

What has all this to do with economic theory? First, much of the argument about the importance of the corporation involves judgments about the degree of competition in industry. For writers like Galbraith, corporations are almost equated to monopoly. However, Galbraith does not suggest that public policy should oppose what he believes is the tendency toward monopoly, because bigness is for him the key to efficiency. The implication of the theory presented earlier, that competition is the most efficient organization of production within an industry, is contradicted by a number of writers.

Secondly, economic theory does not necessarily tell us under what sort of organization people are the happiest.

Jefferson pleaded for an agrarian society of small landowners on the ground that "I think we shall be [virtuous] . . . as long as agriculture is our principal object, which will be the case, while there remains vacant lands in any part of America. When we get piled upon one another in large cities, as in Europe, we shall become corrupt as in Europe, and go to eating one another as they do there." [1] Yet if the people had valued the agrarian life very highly, the pecuniary attractions of the city and industry would not have attracted them in such large numbers. And if a society of craftsmen is more rewarding than an impersonally automated society, would not the competitive system preserve more enterprises of a small scale, even if the earnings of the workers were lower? Some degree of voting for crowded urban living is therefore demonstrated merely by the fact that workers have been willing to locate in cities. The "blind economic forces" that shape our lives do so with at least a small degree of our consent.

The call for revolution stems partly from the view that existing society has too great a degree of inequality to be reformed and partly from the view that happiness would be increased by changing the organization. The New Left favors organizations that would give control to the workers in each enterprise. Yugoslavia has experimented with such reforms in recent years. The state owns the factories but leaves the decisions to the factory committees that are elected by the workers. Profits are divided by the factory among the workers or are allowed to remain with the enterprise. In this system a considerable inequality will

[1] Jefferson to James Madison, Paris, December 20, 1787. Quoted in Adrienne Koch and William Peden, eds., *The Life and Selected Writings of Thomas Jefferson* (New York: Modern Library, 1944), p. 441.

develop among workers in different enterprises according to their efficiency and the opportunities created by demand and competition. Further, inequality may develop within the factory as competition arises for certain scarce skills. These developments may all take place under a socialist organization. The only difference between this system and capitalism is that there will be less property for individuals to hand down by inheritance to future generations.

The fact that workers gain satisfaction from knowing they are working for themselves has not been demonstrated in the cases of British coal miners and Polish industrial workers. Whether a large enterprise is owned by the whole state or by the workers does not seem to affect the monotony of performing repetitive tasks. Large-scale manufacturing is likely to be impersonal regardless of the particular detail of ownership.

One writer of the New Left, Edward Nell, has written of the need to eliminate the market system in a just society. He answers two

common objections to eliminating the market. The first is that material incentives are necessary and/or valuable aids to growth; the second is that different people's preferences must be weighted somehow, since choices have to be made. . . . Material incentives may be useful, but they also have socially harmful effects; moreover, the richer the society the less useful material incentives will be . . . but . . . there will be the same pandering to corrupted tastes, the same tendency for commercial motives to undermine community spirit, the same failure to observe correct priorities.[2]

The "community spirit" will assert itself to give clear indications of consumption and production priorities; indi-

[2] Edward J. Nell, "Automation and the Abolition of the Market," in *Praxis, New Left Notes*, August 7, 1967.

vidual preferences are to be disregarded as subject to "corrupted tastes." A market as a means of organizing group decision-making is not to be trusted in Nell's socialist scheme.

At the same time that Nell was publishing his attack on market organization, a Yugoslav socialist economist, Aleksander Bajt, published an interesting argument calling for the extension of market decision in Yugoslavia, even to the point of creating private property rights in the hands of the workers who presently control, but do not own, the individual enterprises in Yugoslavia.[3] For Bajt, the increasingly complex economics of developed countries cannot be planned efficiently by computers, largely because the trials and errors of economic progress cannot be organized efficiently from a central bureau.

However, the market system in present-day Western countries operates with considerable government intervention. Taxes and welfare subsidies modify the distribution of income provided by the market. Government spending on such services as education, public health, public housing, and roads provides many elements of consumption outside the market. A state where spending in these fields is the government's responsibility has come to be called a welfare state. Intervention in the financial markets controls

---

[3] Aleksander Bajt, in "Property in Capital and in the Means of Production in Socialist Economics," *Journal of Law & Economics,* April 1968, remarks:

> If one wants to develop entrepreneurial activity in socialist enterprises, one has to provide enterprises with adequate legal rights in order to exchange factors and products in as free a manner as possible . . . once you take the independence of enterprises and their entrepreneurial activity, be they individual or collective, seriously . . . it always comes to the situation that enterprises do behave, and the legal structure has to enable them to behave, as if they were owners of the means of production which they use.

the interest rate and the stock of money and thereby modifies the private decisions of the market.

Economics provides a framework of analysis of group decision-making through what is called the market. Political science has traditionally studied group decision-making through elections and representative governmental institutions. As this book is written, "Student leaders from 10 countries, appearing on a British television program . . . [are denouncing] elections as a means of bringing about change and expressing the will of the people." [4] The many economic and political organizations that have been tried in the world of the twentieth century have all employed markets in making allocation decisions. It would be foolish to ignore the principles of market economics when reforming any of these many systems.

[4] "Student Leaders, on British TV, Assail Voting," *The New York Times,* June 14, 1968, p. 2.

Suggestions for Further Reading

Chapter I

Knight, F. H. *The Economic Organization*. New York: Harper Torchbooks, 1965.

Lerner, Abba P. *Everybody's Business: A Re-examination of Current Assumptions in Economics and Public Policy*. New York: Harper Torchbooks, 1961.

Chapter II

Knight, F. H. *The Economic Organization*. New York: Harper Torchbooks, chap. ii.

Schumpeter, Joseph. *Theory of Economic Development*. New York: Galaxy Books, 1961.

Chapter III

Shackle, George L. S. *Economics for Pleasure*. (Books I and II.) New York: Cambridge University Press, 1959.

Chapter IV

Friedman, Milton. "Inflation: Causes and Consequences," in *Dollars and Deficits, Inflation, Monetary Policy and the Balance of Payments*. Englewood Cliffs, N.J.: Prentice-Hall, 1968.

Haberler, G. *Inflation: Its Causes and Cures*. Washington, D.C.: American Enterprise Institute for Public Policy Research, 1966.

Harrod, R. F. *Life of John Maynard Keynes*. New York: Harcourt, Brace & World, 1951.

Mundell, R. *Man and Economics*. New York: McGraw-Hill, 1968, pp. 85–115.

Chapter V

Ashton, Thomas S. *The Industrial Revolution, 1760–1830.* New York: Galaxy Books, 1964.

Friedman, Milton. *Capitalism and Freedom.* Chicago: Phoenix Books, 1963, chap. x.

Maddison, Angus. *Economic Growth in the West: Comparative Experience in Europe and North America.* New York: The Twentieth Century Fund, 1964, chap. i.

Rees, Albert. *The Economics of Trade Unions.* Chicago: University of Chicago Press, 1962.

Smith, Adam. *Wealth of Nations.* (Book I.) New York: Modern Library, 1937.

Wright, D. M. (ed.). *The Impact of the Union.* New York: Augustus M. Kelley, 1966.

Chapter VI

Mundell, R. *Man and Economics.* New York: McGraw-Hill, 1968, pp. 117–152.

Chapter VIII

Galbraith, John K. *The New Industrial State.* Boston: Houghton Mifflin, 1967.

Schumpeter, Joseph. *Capitalism, Socialism and Democracy.* New York: Harper & Row, 1950.

Simons, Henry C. *Economic Policy for a Free Society.* Chicago: University of Chicago Press, 1948.

Smith, Adam. *Wealth of Nations.* New York: Modern Library, 1937.

Index